Justin's mum:
'Every time you cook Justin, I find this
tiny bit of Indian in there.'

Justin:
'Wait, you think everything I cook
is Indian?'

Justin's mum:
'Yes!'

Justin:
'That's so funny. Because when you cook, even if
you're making pasta or lasagne, I always joke that
it tastes like curry because of all the ginger and
garlic. And you think now my cooking is like that?'

Justin's mum:
'Well, not all of it, but most of it. You either
use Indian spice or something in there. I like the
way you can bring things together and create these
amazing flavours, so a little piece of you comes
along with whatever you make. I could eat your
cooking every day.'

Justin:
'Thanks Mum.'

Justin's mum:
'But I still like my chicken curry more.'

JUSTIN NARAYAN
WITH NICHOLAS JORDAN

EVERYTHING IS INDIAN

murdoch books
Sydney | London

CONTENTS

TWO

LOVE, ENTERTAINMENT, HUNGER, PRESSURE: EVERYTHING THAT MADE ME COOK

THREE

I GREW UP VERY CONFUSED: MAYBE WE'RE NOT THAT DIFFERENT

RECIPE GUIDE

Thank you for picking up this book. I dreamt about this happening — being on TV, writing my own cookbook, having a restaurant. Pretty much everything I saw Jamie Oliver do. But now it's a reality and it's very surreal. I know it wouldn't have happened without the person at the other end of this book: you. If it wasn't for you, all of these recipes and stories would just be Google Docs I'd send to my mate Rob. So I just wanted to say thanks for giving me the privilege of sharing my story and recipes. I am extremely grateful.

'When you acknowledge, as you must, that there is no such thing as perfect food, only the idea of it, then the real purpose of striving toward perfection becomes clear: to make people happy, that is what cooking is all about.'

Thomas Keller, The French Laundry Cookbook

When you first look at a recipe or think about cooking, I don't want you to think about how to make it tasty. I want you to think about how to make someone happy. Think about who you're cooking for rather than what you're cooking. Whoever that person is, they are more important than what you cook. Food is just a way to connect with them and make them feel something. That is how my mum and my parti (grandma) cooked. If I'm coming over, Mum is cooking my favourite dish, chicken curry. If it's my brother, she's making prawn curry, even though she can't even eat prawns (she's allergic). If someone new is coming over, she'll want to know what they like and what they can't eat. She'll go easy on the spice, but lay out all the chutneys and pickles so people can still go hard on spice and extra flavour if they want. There is no ego in their cooking, it's not in their DNA at all. They are always making food for others, trying to make people happy and building community. That's what I want to do and that's what I want to encourage you to do. For me, cooking, writing recipes and making this book has never been about the food, it's been about connecting with other people.

I'm not saying that food is the only way to connect ... you might do it through dance, sport, art or whatever, but everyone relates to food. Everyone eats and shares food; it's part of what makes us human. We are the only animals that cook. Cooking food was important in our development as a species, and it helped us form our communities, relationships and family units. Communities revolve around people, but food is so often the glue connecting it all. We can be from different cultures and different sides of the world. We can disagree on just about everything, but when we cook for each other and share a meal, we have everything in common.

Cooking and sharing food brings us together — it's affection, it's care, it's community and it reinforces what it means to be human. And I think now we're missing that, more than we realise. We're separated by screens, jobs, distance and whatever else life throws at us, and we don't always have the dinner table to reunite us. I feel like it's becoming rare to sit around a table together, and I think we're lacking a sense of community because of that.

This cookbook isn't the answer but, if anything, I hope one of the stories and recipes inside can be part of the answer. What I hope is for this book to inspire you to make just one meal for someone else. Just take one recipe and share what you make with someone. It doesn't even need to be a recipe; it could just be a story or a picture that gets you inspired. It doesn't even matter if it's a fail. What that person will remember is that you invited them over, cooked for them and you shared a meal together. You may not make something mind-blowing — not every meal I make is a culinary masterpiece, sometimes it's just food — but you will at least make a memory. So, just one meal with one other person, one attempt, that's all I'm asking.

The recipes in this book are about me, my culture and where I come from. Food is how I relate to the world and these recipes are how I've related to the people around me. It starts with the Fijian-Indian recipes I grew up with (traditional and easy versions you can make in around 30 minutes), then it goes into all the dishes I've learned to cook growing up in Australia. It's a melting pot of cultures here — when it comes to food, I think Australia is one of the best places in the world — and that mix of cultures is a part of me. It's part of who I am and it's inspired me. So, it might look like this book has recipes from all over the world, but none of these recipes are inspired by my travels. They're inspired by the Fijian and Indian food from my family, the Chinese restaurants in Nedlands, the garlic sauce in Granville, the Portuguese chicken in Petersham, and all the people I grew up with.

When I think about the Chinese dishes I had in Perth, I think about chop suey from Fiji; when I eat garlic sauce, I remember the garlic my mum uses in all her curries; and sometimes when I eat Portuguese chicken with my mum, she will say, 'If we add some cumin and chilli, this would be like a curry.' These foods are all part of me. That's where the title comes from: *Everything is Indian*. I know everything isn't Indian, but it's my world, it's the start of everything. It's why I think about making caramel slice with cardamom and nutmeg, and roast potatoes with turmeric and mustard seeds — that's my style of food. I'm using Indian food to relate to your cuisine and your world, and I hope you can do the same. Take my dishes and interpret them with your own culture and experience.

All of these dishes are designed for you to share with other people. They're also designed to be as easy as possible, because the most important thing about food is that it brings people together.

Fake It Till You Make It: Basic Tips to Be a Good Cook

Anyone can cook, even if they think they can't. It's like dancing. There are people who refuse to dance. They just think, 'Oh, I don't dance' (I'm one of those people). But they'll still bob their head and sway from side to side. If you can make instant noodles, you can cook. Everyone starts somewhere.

The recipes in this book are designed for a home cook to achieve a restaurant-quality meal or the standard of an authentic Indian grandma's cooking with domestic equipment and ingredients. It's generally simple, straightforward cooking that doesn't take a lot of time. In other words, the time to flavour pay-off is high.

FOLLOWING RECIPES

If you want to follow to a tee and replicate exactly what I've put, you can. But if you want to take some liberty with a recipe, substitute ingredients or be creative, I give full permission — use the recipes as your springboard. Generally when you're following a recipe, read the entire thing first, prepare your mise en place (more on that later) and make sure you have a clean workspace.

MAKE IT EASY

My parti (grandma) would spend hours cooking. She would break down a whole chicken for a curry, make fresh roti for every meal, turn home-grown vegetables into pickles and spend hours over the stove making five or six dishes for our family or any random guest who came in unexpectedly. But the world doesn't work like that anymore. Everyone is busy. What I've tried to do is find easier ways to prep things, so I can still enjoy the flavours and memories of my mum and parti's cooking. I know roast chicken curry and masala roast potatoes aren't exactly the same as what Parti made, but I can have them on the table on a weeknight. I know if someone came over they would still feel the same amount of love and effort.

My basic theory for cooking is: make it easy. You don't want to have to put in the same amount of effort as they do at a restaurant, but I think you can still achieve the same amount of flavour. Most of my recipes take less than an hour of 'active' cooking time. I've also given suggestions for easy ways to do things. I'm busy, you're busy, that's life. If you want to chuck the dhal in a slow cooker, use store-bought roti or sub in frozen chopped veg, do these things.

SEASONING AND TASTING

A lot of recipes will tell you to add a pinch of salt, but pinches come in all shapes and sizes. I measured my pinch, and it's about ½ teaspoon (about 2 g).

Adding salt — it can be salt, soy, anchovies, fish sauce, etc. — should happen while the food is cooking. In general, the longer salt is in contact with an ingredient, the better it's absorbed. Taste, then season as you go. Do one last taste at the end to see if you need to adjust. If you're not confident seasoning, go light to begin with and add more in at the end.

GBD

You'll hear me say GBD a lot. It stands for golden brown and delicious. It's my nickname (that's a lame joke, but I hope it got a reaction). Golden brown is the colour you want when you cook meat and vegetables. The browning process — called the Maillard reaction — is a chemical reaction that occurs when proteins and sugars are transformed by heat, creating new flavours and aromas. It adds a heap of depth and complexity. Imagine the difference between a boiled chicken breast and a charred, barbecued one: that's the Maillard reaction. The enemy of GBD is moisture, aka water. And the enemy of water is the paper towel. Always use one to remove moisture from your protein or vegetable before cooking. You have to cook with high heat. The ideal temperature for browning is 140–165°C (275–310°F). Seasoning and GBD are the two best things you can do to make something tasty.

EQUIPMENT

You can make most of these recipes with just a good quality frying pan and a stick blender. If you want to upgrade, spend your money on these: a cast iron pan, a good chef's knife and a heavy-based saucepan with a lid. They will last a really long time — maybe even forever — and if you get these three things, you'll want to cook; it'll feel sexy. The next most important things are, in no particular order: a whisk, a spatula, a few mixing bowls, a good chopping board (I like to use synthetic rubber) and a food processor. That's all you need to make everything in this book (and most recipes, in general).

OVEN TEMPERATURES

All the oven temperatures in this book are using the fan-forced setting. Unlike commercial ovens, which are very consistent, domestic ovens can vary by 5–10°C (10–25°F). That's why the recipes have varying times and tips for what to look for. When you learn to spot the jiggle of a crème brûlée or the feel of a perfect roast chicken, you'll be able to cook in any oven.

MISE EN PLACE (PUTTING IN PLACE)

This basically means prep. Have everything you need for each step measured and put in individual vessels, ready to be added in. That way you don't have to take an extra second scraping something off a cutting board. You want to move quickly and be in the flow.

As you learn recipes and progress as a cook, you will learn to chop, measure and add spice as you go. If you really want to be fast and finish a meal in 15 or 20 minutes, this is how you have to do it. But when you're starting out, have everything cut, measured out and ready to go. Make it easy.

TEASPOONS AND TABLESPOONS

All of my tablespoon and teaspoon measurements are with regular kitchen spoons, and I'm just eyeing the amount. Measuring half a teaspoon is annoying and takes a lot of time, and the difference between an accurately measured teaspoon and a rough guess is negligible. But if you want to use precise measuring devices, go nuts. The only time I use them is for baking. That's a bit more exact. For savoury food, I can't justify it — you can just use a standard tablespoon or teaspoon.

If you can make
instant noodles,
you can cook.
Everyone starts
somewhere.

A Different Way to Think About Cooking

People are always asking me for general cooking tips. These are the tips I give them. This is a framework to make any dish from any cuisine tasty. It's also a way to think about food and understand what makes good food.

LEVEL ONE: TASTE

<u>THEORY:</u> The first level is making sure whatever you're cooking tastes good — wow. The basis to this is understanding the five tastes: salty, sweet, sour, bitter and umami (savouriness). Try and think about which ingredients are providing which tastes, and how your cooking techniques will affect the balance. If you nail that, you'll be able to create tasty dishes consistently. Ninety per cent of my cooking — mostly midweek meals where I'm cooking for sustenance — is just aiming for level one.

<u>PRACTICE:</u> Try making a simple salad dressing with mustard, olive oil, vinegar, salt and honey. That has pretty much all the flavours. Taste it as you add each ingredient and try to find the right balance. I find going too far with the salt (or any of the ingredients) is good practice to know what the limit is, then add more of the other ingredients to balance it.

LEVEL TWO: TEXTURE AND SENSATION

<u>THEORY:</u> Once you know you can nail the taste of a dish, think about texture: crunchy, creamy, chewy, fatty, gelatinous, etc. Think about textural variance and what techniques and ingredients you can use to enhance or change the texture of your dish. The best horror films also make you laugh. That's what you want with texture — contrasting or opposing elements. Think creamy with crunchy, or wet with dry. Sensation is a subcategory of this — chilli and temperature are sensations. Just consider which ones you want and how they will affect your dish.

<u>PRACTICE:</u> Get some ice-cream, two bowls and put a scoop in each bowl. Drizzle some smooth peanut butter on one scoop. That's soft on soft. For the other, drop over an equal amount of roughly chopped roasted, salted peanuts. That's crunchy on soft. You have the exact same ingredients — peanuts and ice-cream — but see how the texture affects

the flavour and experience of the dish. Now, combine both scoops and see how having layers of texture impacts the dish. Great dessert; I would smash that right now.

LEVEL THREE: VISUAL

THEORY: This should never be the first thing you think about, but if you know you can nail the taste and texture of a dish, bringing this in will have a big impact on your guests' experience. If I'm having people over or trying to impress a loved one, I'm thinking about all three levels.

PRACTICE: This is more up to interpretation and preference, but a couple of general tips: play with colour, height (literally, is it flat or tall?), different textures, garnishes and the plate you use. Try plating contrasting colours, using different coloured ingredients or a different coloured plate, and having odd numbers on the plate (for some reason that can be pleasing to the eye — it's a thing, check out the rule of odds).

LEVEL FOUR: MEMORY AND EXPERIENCE

THEORY: At the highest level of cooking — what they do in really good restaurants — is the manipulation of memories, nostalgia and experience. You don't have to nail all four levels to make good food, but if you want to create an incredible experience for people, you have to consider every level.

PRACTICE: Number one, ask your guests what they like and don't like. Two, cook something nostalgic for them, make something that tells a story or, better, incorporate a bit of flavour from your life or culture with something from your guest's life (eg the barfi-spiced caramel slice on page 124).

ONE

THE FAMILY HOUSE

My grandparents, Parti and Tata, lived with us when I was growing up. Mum and Parti were always in the kitchen. Often when I woke up, Mum would be cooking breakfast, preparing something for lunch or dinner, or making something to take to someone's house. When they weren't working, Dad and Tata would be in the garden, watering plants, tending to the chillies and beans or just digging a hole for something. If not, Dad would be watching the news, Mum would be watching a Bollywood film, and Parti, Tata and I would be watching cooking shows. You could predict it exactly.

Our door was always open or unlocked, because you never knew when someone would pop in for tea. On the weekends or after I got home from school, it would be like every five seconds an uncle, auntie or one of my grandparents' friends would just drop in — there was always family in town. Often it would be someone I didn't even know. Sometimes they'd visit just to say hi, and sometimes they would have a huge bag of cumquats or whatever they were growing in their garden. They'd be coming over to drop the produce off, but they'd never just do that.

Whenever a guest walked in, there would be this funny joust at the doorstep:

'Don't worry, leave your shoes on.'

'Oh, no no, I'll take them off.'

'No, don't worry, it's dirty in here anyway.' (This is what Mum would say after spending the last hour cleaning the house.)

'No, it's okay, I can take them off.'

Everyone would know full well the guests were going to end up taking their shoes off, but there would always be the same exchange. Then they walk in, sit in the lounge room and someone asks them what they want. It's never 'Do you want?' but always 'What do you want?'. Then there's another joust:

'Tea, coffee?'

'Oh, na, na I'm fine, I don't want anything.'

'I've already put the kettle on. Which do you want?'

'No really, it's fine, I'm okay.'

Eventually, they just tell you what they want and if they don't, they'll get something anyway. Usually, all the men will gravitate to the couch while Parti or Mum whips something up — murukku, samosa (we always had handmade samosa in the freezer for when guests came over) or a packet of Arnott's Assorted. I was introverted, so I would be helping in the kitchen. My brother would be chatting with the guests or putting biscuits or bhuja mix on the table.

We'd give them a little plate of food, which was like a meal in itself, and a tea or coffee. They'd always say 'no', but we'd tell them, 'Don't worry, just leave whatever you don't eat on the plate.' They'd always end up finishing it.

Then — and this would always happen — someone in my family would ask, 'Why don't you just stay for dinner?' Then, another joust happens:

'Oh no no, we have to Go.' (Subtext: I don't want to be a hassle.)

'Just have a little bit to eat.' (Subtext: There is no such thing as a little bit. If we can get you to the dinner table, we know you're staying for dinner.)

'Oh no, we don't want to be a hassle. You don't need to cater for us.' (Subtext: None.)

'It's no hassle at all.' (Subtext: We are literally prepared for this exact situation. There is no such thing as a curry for two.)

We were always prepared for this. Mum bought extra groceries and cooked extra food, just in case. In the laundry freezer (we had more than one freezer and an extra fridge — you know, just in case the apocalypse came) there were containers of curries, khatta bhaji and miscellaneous cuts of fish and meat. They all looked the same, but Mum would know what each one was. There was an outdoor kitchen for making more pungent curries, seafood and deep frying. The inside kitchen was used for dhal, rice and roti. The cupboards would be full of condiments — mango pickles, lemon pickles, chilli chutney, tamarind chutney ... at any given time there'd be at least ten made and ready to go. Whenever someone came over unexpectedly, Mum was prepared.

The kids would be setting the table and, because guests are here, we're getting the good plates out. The pinnacle for us was the Corningware. If you weren't doing your job for some reason, you knew you were in trouble later. We were well trained.

Mum's cooking would be insane. She would ask you what you like or what you don't eat and she would always cater to that. It was never just one curry. There would be a minimum of three, plus rice, freshly made roti, condiments and pickles. For regular family dinners we'd have egg curry, bean curry, chickpea curry and tinned fish curry, but guests would get the premium ingredients — prawns, crab, chicken and lamb. At the time I never thought about it like that. To me there were no cheap or expensive curries; it was all delicious, but that's what we did. We wanted to treat guests well.

The night would end with more tea, as well as some sweets or cut-up fresh fruit, and sometimes tinned fruit with ice-cream or evaporated milk poured on top, like a milky fruit salad soup. If Tata was there, there would be whisky too. Then the guests would leave with containers of leftovers and a bag of beans, chilli, corn or whatever we were growing in the garden.

For my mum and dad, this was just normal.

When I was about 13, my family lost everything. In the space of two years, we went from having a big house and fancy cars to having zero, Dad being sick and at home, and Mum working night shifts packing boxes in a factory. It was a dramatic change. What I remember most is that the hospitality never changed. Neither did the way my parents entertained guests and the way my mum cooked. It was always nourishing and delicious. We were just having fewer prawn curries and more egg ones. Despite everything that happened, it always felt like there was abundance at the dinner table. If someone came over, or even if it was just the family, the standard never dropped.

I even remember Mum cooking for 30 people once; there were like eight different curries on the table. I also remember her making food for tradies coming over. I'd see her in the kitchen making something and ask, 'Mum, what are you doing?' She'd just say, 'I'm making something for Mike, the electrician. He's coming over.' It didn't matter who they were, and it didn't matter whether we were rich, poor or whatever, Mum and Dad always showed generosity through food. That was their way to connect with people. That philosophy was who they were.

As a kid, I had a love/hate relationship with my family's open-door policy. As a teen, I hated it. I wanted my own space and privacy, and I also saw how much my parents were sacrificing. Why are they spending so much money on this stranger? Why are they spending so much energy on other people? I thought Dad should be prioritising his health, not late-night airport runs for whatever random relative or friend was staying over. I wanted them to focus on the family, themselves and their health. At times I was angry at them for not doing that.

Now I really admire and respect my parents for how they treat people. The ironic thing is, I reckon now I'm exactly like them. My wife Esther and I have people over all the time — at least once a week. Every time a neighbour pops by, I'm like, 'Come in!' Sometimes I give them a container of food to take home. I always have something I can whip up in two seconds to give them.

I'm wired just like my parents.

Masala Chai

MAKES 4–5 CUPS (1–1.25 LITRES) × ACTIVE TIME 10 MINUTES × TOTAL TIME 20 MINUTES

I went to India for the first time in 2017. It was confusing being there. I look Indian, but I was born and raised in Australia — am I Australian, am I Fijian, am I Indian? I was displaced. But there was one thing that always made me feel like I fit in. On every block, around every corner, there would be a chai stall. Tuktuk drivers would be there sipping chai with kids on their way to school and guys who'd roll up in fancy cars and suits. Every time I went into someone's home or a restaurant, I'd be offered chai — in the morning, at night, it was always time for a cup of chai. I remember that first sip in India and thinking, this is the best thing I've ever tasted. It was a completely different experience, but it was like I was having chai at home with Mum.

It's such a pivotal part of Indian food and culture, and it's a pivotal part of whatever my culture is. At my house, you always know a guest is coming over because Mum has a pot on the boil. If anyone comes in unexpectedly, they're invited in for tea. And it's never just a teabag in a cup. It's always made like this, with so much effort and energy. Chai for me is home. It's as powerful for me as chicken curry; it reminds me of who I am and how I want to treat people.

30 g (1 oz) fresh ginger,
    roughly chopped
    (fine to leave skin on)
1 teaspoon green cardamom
    pods, lightly crushed
    (use a pestle, rolling pin
    or the side of a knife)
½ teaspoon whole cloves
½ teaspoon whole black
    peppercorns
1 large cinnamon stick
1 teaspoon vanilla bean paste
    or ½ vanilla pod
1 heaped teaspoon
    fennel seeds
25 g (1 oz) loose Ceylon
    or Assam tea leaves
    (or 7 teabags)
3 cups (750 ml) milk (see tip)
40 g (1½ oz) soft brown sugar,
    plus extra to taste

Place everything, except the milk and sugar, in a saucepan with 2 cups (500 ml) water. Bring to the boil, reduce heat and simmer for 5 minutes.

Add the milk and sugar, bring back to a simmer, then stir constantly as it simmers. Taste and add more sugar, if needed. After 5 minutes turn off the heat and let it sit for another 5–10 minutes.

Strain into a teapot or directly into cups and sip away.

TIP Good milk makes a good chai. In Fiji, they use milk straight from the cow; it's warm, it probably has a hint of grassiness, heaps of fat and is super thick. Here, Jersey milk is the closest thing you can get. Also, don't be afraid to boil it. In Western cooking, you never let milk boil because it develops a skin, but in Indian cooking, you boil the shit out of it. I hate the skin, but that's how you know you have a good chai.

Murukku

MAKES 80–100 PIECES × ACTIVE/TOTAL TIME 1 HOUR

Murukku are star-shaped, crunchy, savoury snacks. You can buy them at most Indian shops, but they're a bit different to the homemade version. Mum's have that perfect crunch, like a potato chip — they just disintegrate when you eat them. The ones in the store are a bit harder. Every family has their own recipe, but Mum is famous for hers.

Full disclaimer: You need a special murukku device to make this. Otherwise, you can't get the right shape. Maybe this will be a recipe no one ever makes, but I'm writing it down to preserve it for my family. If there is one person who goes out, buys a murukku device and makes it, that'll be amazing. Shoot me a DM, we'll do something to celebrate. I don't know what, but it'll be something.

'We'd all Get together at Justin's house for a board Game night and she would make murukku and chai with all the spices. I'll never forget it. She also Gave my wife Amanda and I ziplock baGs of them, but Amanda rarely Got any as I would literally finish them off on the drive home. They're that Good.'

— Justin's mate Rob

3 cups (400 g) fine rice flour
1 cup (100 g) chickpea flour
  (besan)
1½ teaspoons salt
1 teaspoon chilli powder
1 teaspoon ajwain (also known
  as caraway or carom seeds)
1 tablespoon cumin seeds
1 tablespoon sesame seeds
60 g (2¼ oz) unsalted butter,
  melted
Canola oil, for deep-frying

Mix all the dry ingredients in a large bowl. Add the melted butter and mix using your hands until you get a sandy, crumb-like texture. Gradually add 2¼ cups (560 ml) water and mix until combined and you have a soft, cookie dough-like consistency.

Heat the oil in a cast iron frying pan over medium heat or a deep fryer to 170–180°C (340–360°F). (If you don't have a probe, put a wooden spoon in the oil. If small bubbles appear around the spoon, it's ready.) Line a plate with paper towel.

Using a murukku device with the star-shaped extruder, push the dough through the device directly into the oil, creating small, flat spiral shapes. Fry until golden, about 2–3 minutes each side. Drain on the paper towel-lined plate and allow them to cool.

Either eat them all or place them in an airtight container — they'll keep for 4 weeks at room temperature.

Murukku (page 25)

Masala Chai (page 24)

How to Cook Perfect Rice

1 CUP (200 G) UNCOOKED RICE SERVES 2 WITH SOME LEFT OVER
ACTIVE TIME 5 MINUTES × TOTAL TIME 35 MINUTES

I didn't start cooking rice until I was in my mid-20s, after I'd learned to cook pretty much everything else. Even though it's the easiest thing ever, I stuffed it up so many times — everyone says this is crazy, but I didn't have a rice cooker. When I nailed it, it gave me a lot of confidence. Years later, I still don't have a rice cooker. I'm not a minimalist or anything, but single-use appliances annoy me. Besides, you can get a great result in a saucepan. The only thing rice cookers do is save you 5 minutes at the start.

The perfect rice should be fluffy, the grains should be separate and they should hold their shape, but not have much bite. I usually get aged basmati or jasmine. Perfect rice doesn't make a dish, but if you nail this, you're halfway there.

RATIOS (RICE:WATER)
jasmine or basmati 1:2
sushi 1:1.5

Wash the rice until the water runs clear. (This removes starch, which is essential for making fluffy rice.) Drain the rice, then put in a saucepan with the water using the ratio on the left. Bring to a simmer — this will take about 5 minutes. As soon as it comes to a simmer, turn the heat to low and cover with a lid. Let it cook for 15 minutes (the same time for any amount of rice).

Turn off the heat and let it sit for another 10–15 minutes (don't touch it, keep that lid on). Once the timer is up, you have perfect rice and now you can do anything in life.

TIP If you do have a rice cooker, you can use the same ratios.

Savoury Steamed Semolina Cake (Dhokla)

SERVES 6–8 × ACTIVE TIME 10 MINUTES × TOTAL TIME 40 MINUTES

Dhokla is a steamed, savoury semolina kind-of-pudding, kind-of-cake thing. There are so many different versions of it; some are sweet and some are finished with onion, chilli and garlic. This is Mum's recipe, which is a bit more soft and delicate. We'd usually have it with yoghurt and mint chutney, and serve it with tea as a little pre-dinner snack. I've given you the option to steam it (the more traditional method) or use the microwave like Mum does.

2 tablespoons ghee
½ brown onion, finely chopped
1–2 bird's eye chillies,
    thinly sliced
¼ teaspoon mustard seeds
5–6 fresh curry leaves,
    roughly chopped
½ teaspoon ground turmeric
1 cup (180 g) coarse semolina
1 cup (260 g) plain yoghurt
½ cup (125 ml) milk
2 teaspoons Eno Fruit Salt
    Regular (see tip)

TO SERVE
1 small bunch of fresh
    coriander (cilantro), leaves
    picked and chopped
Coriander, Mint and Yoghurt
    Chutney (page 224)

Heat the ghee in a frying pan over high heat. When it's melted and hot, add the onion, chilli, mustard seeds and curry leaves. Cook until the onion is golden, about 3–5 minutes. Add the turmeric and a generous pinch of salt, mix, then turn off the heat. Transfer the spiced onion mixture to a bowl. Mix in the semolina, then add the yoghurt and milk. Mix well. (It should resemble a thick cake batter.)

OPTION 1: STEAM
Place a wire rack in a wok or large saucepan, then pour in some water (reaching just below the rack). Heat until it's lightly simmering. Line the base of a 22 cm (8½ inch) springform cake tin (a regular cake tin works too, springform is just easier) with baking paper, then lightly grease the base and side with oil. When you're ready to cook, add the fruit salt to the mixture and stir to combine (it will aerate and froth at this point). Pour the mixture into the prepared tin and spread it evenly. Place the tin on top of the rack in the wok to steam (you can put the tin in a steaming basket if you have one). Cook over a gentle steam until a toothpick inserted into the centre comes out clean and the cake springs back after you give it a press, about 20–25 minutes.

OPTION 2: MICROWAVE
Lightly grease the base and side of a microwave-safe dish. When you're ready to cook, add the fruit salt to the mixture and stir to combine (it will aerate and froth at this point). Pour the mixture into the prepared dish. Cover with plastic wrap and microwave until a toothpick inserted into the centre comes out clean and the cake springs back after you give it a press, about 8–10 minutes.

Let the cake settle for 5 minutes, then slice into squares and serve with coriander and chutney.

TIP Eno Fruit Salt is a weird ingredient that I only use for this. It's basically used to settle your stomach. If you don't want to buy it, you can use 1½ teaspoons bicarbonate of soda (baking soda) and ¼ teaspoon citric acid.

Samosa

MAKES 26 × ACTIVE/TOTAL TIME 1 HOUR + 1 HOUR COOLING

Samosa and sausage rolls were the pinnacle teatime snacks for me. We'd always have a container of both in the freezer ready to go in case someone unexpectedly dropped in. I think the first time Mum and Parti (Grandma) invited me into their octagon (aka the kitchen) was to help make samosa. I was ten or eleven and it was me, Parti and Mum in a production line, chatting, bonding and having little nibbles of the stuffing. It's like the scene in *Crazy Rich Asians* when they're all folding dumplings, only Indian.

Neutral high smoke point oil, for deep-frying

SAMOSA FILLING
2 large potatoes
¼ cup (60 ml) light olive oil
1 teaspoon The Mixture (page 60) or ¼ teaspoon each of cumin seeds and black mustard seeds, and ⅛ teaspoon fenugreek seeds
1 sprig fresh curry leaves, finely chopped
1–2 garlic cloves, crushed, or 1 teaspoon garlic paste (page 59)
1 teaspoon ground turmeric
¼ teaspoon chilli powder
1 teaspoon ground cumin
1 cup (150 g) frozen mixed vegetables (or a mix of carrots, corn and peas)
1 small bunch of fresh coriander (cilantro), leaves picked and roughly chopped

SAMOSA PASTRY
2 cups (300 g) plain (all-purpose) flour, plus extra 3 tablespoons and for dusting
¼ teaspoon cumin seeds
20–25 fresh curry leaves, finely chopped
2 tablespoons light olive oil

TO SERVE
Fresh Coriander Chutney (page 224), store-bought tamarind chutney or tomato sauce mixed with a few dashes of Tabasco
Fried curry leaves (optional)

To make the samosa filling, peel and slice the potatoes into small cubes, then put them in a bowl of water (this prevents oxidisation). Heat the olive oil in a saucepan over medium heat. Add the whole spices and curry leaves and cook for about 1 minute. Add the garlic and cook for a further minute. Add the powdered spices and a pinch of salt and cook for 30 seconds. Drain the potatoes, then add to the spice mixture and mix well. Cover and let it cook over medium heat, while periodically stirring, for 15 minutes. Now, add the frozen vegetables and cook until the potatoes are soft, about 10–15 minutes. Turn off the heat, add the coriander and season with salt to taste. Allow to cool down to room temperature. Now is a great time to make the pastry.

To make the pastry, place the flour, cumin seeds, curry leaves and a pinch of salt in a large bowl. Add the olive oil and mix — you'll get a crumbly, sand-like texture. Add ¾ cup (185 ml) room-temperature water and knead the dough on a clean work surface until you get a smooth dough, adding more water as required — this will take 5–10 minutes. Divide the dough into eight equal pieces and shape each into a little ball. Dusting with extra flour as needed, roll each ball into a flat circle, aiming for about 1–2 mm (¹⁄₁₆ inch) thick (like a roti or tortilla). Heat a frying pan over medium heat, then cook each pastry for about 10 seconds each side. Once they're all cooked, slice them into quarters, so you have mini triangles with a curved edge (like little pizza slices).

Combine the extra 3 tablespoons flour with ¼ cup (60 ml) water in a bowl to form the dough glue. Now, to make the samosa shape, with the curved edge closest to you, overlap the straight sides to create a funnel, then seal with a little dough glue. Stuff the cavity with the filling until full. Fold the top down to enclose the filling and seal with some more dough glue.

Heat the neutral oil in a cast iron frying pan over medium heat or a deep fryer to 170–180°C (340–360°F). (If you don't have a probe, put a wooden spoon in the oil. If small bubbles appear around the spoon, it's ready.) Line a plate with paper towel.

In batches, deep-fry the samosa until golden, about 5–8 minutes. Drain the finished samosa on the paper towel-lined plate.

Serve with chutney or Tabasco tomato sauce, garnished with fried curry leaves, if using, and a cup of tea.

TIP These freeze really well. Just place the raw, filled samosa on a tray and freeze. When they're solid, place them in a ziplock bag in the freezer. To cook, thaw, then deep-fry.

Cassava Chips

Taro Chips (Crisps)
(page 34)

Cassava Chips

SERVES 4–6 (MAKES 900 G/2 LB) × ACTIVE TIME 25 MINUTES × TOTAL TIME 55 MINUTES

These were the ultimate after-school snack, like a denser, creamier, crisper potato chip — I'm talking fish and chip style, not crisps. Parti (Grandma) or Mum would fry them up when we got home and we'd eat them with chutney or tomato sauce (tomato sauce with some Tabasco in there is a sick move) — arguably the best way to eat cassava, although I'm not sure who the argument is with.

1 kg (2 lb 4 oz) frozen
   or fresh cassava
Neutral high smoke point oil,
   for deep-frying
1–2 tablespoons plain
   (all-purpose) flour

SEASONING
½ teaspoon salt or
   Chicken Salt (page 229)
½ teaspoon ground turmeric
¼ teaspoon chilli powder
½ teaspoon ground cumin

TO SERVE
Fresh Coriander Chutney
   (page 224), Coriander,
   Mint and Yoghurt Chutney
   (page 224) and/or
   Flavoured Mayo (page 227)

Place the cassava in a saucepan of cold, salted water and bring to the boil, then reduce the heat and simmer until cooked through (you should be able to slide a fork through), about 20 minutes. Drain and allow to cool and dry. Once cooled, slice the cassava into chips (I do fingers 1–2 cm/½–¾ inch thick). Discard any fibrous, stringy bits.

Combine all the seasoning ingredients in a small bowl.

Heat the oil in a cast iron frying pan over medium heat or a deep fryer to 170–180°C (340–360°F). (If you don't have a probe, put a wooden spoon in the oil. If small bubbles appear around the spoon, it's ready.) Line a plate with paper towel.

Toss the cassava in enough flour to fully coat, then deep-fry, in batches, until golden brown and crispy, about 2–5 minutes. (You don't want to overcrowd or the oil will lose too much heat.) Drain the finished cassava on the paper towel-lined plate, then place in a bowl. Hit them (they should still be hot) with the seasoning and toss.

Serve with chutney and/or mayo.

Taro Chips (Crisps)

SERVES 4 (MAKES 400 G/14 OZ) × ACTIVE/TOTAL TIME 20 MINUTES

This wasn't something I grew up with, but I did grow up with potato chips (or crisps if that's your thing) and I did grow up with taro. We'd usually have it boiled or, if we were lucky, boiled then fried, so it was a taro chip kind of thing (like an actual fish and chip, chip). I wanted to know if you could shave it, deep-fry it and turn it into a chip (the other kind of chip, the crisp kind). I know this is a big call, but I think taro makes the superior chip. The starch helps it stay crisp for longer and there's more depth of flavour and a slight sweetness.

200–400 g (7–14 oz) fresh taro
Neutral high smoke point oil,
    for deep-frying

SEASONING
Chicken Salt (page 229)
OR
Fine salt
OR
½ teaspoon ground cumin
¼ teaspoon smoked paprika
¼ teaspoon chilli powder
½ teaspoon salt

Peel the taro, then slice, using a mandolin or some impressive knife skills, into very thin slices and place in a bowl of cold water.

Heat the oil in a cast iron frying pan over medium heat or a deep fryer to 170–180°C (340–360°F). (If you don't have a probe, put a wooden spoon in the oil. If small bubbles appear around the spoon, it's ready.) Line a plate with paper towel.

Dry the taro completely using a clean tea (dish) towel. In small batches, add the taro to the oil. (You don't want to overcrowd or the oil will lose too much heat.) Fry until very lightly golden brown, about 2–5 minutes each batch. Drain on the paper towel-lined plate as you go.

When you've finished frying and the chips are still hot, put them in a bowl with a generous amount of seasoning and toss.

As pictured on page 32

I don't know if they make this in India or not. It is just our cooking.

Fried Eggs with Roti

SERVES 2 (MAKES 4 ROTI) × ACTIVE/TOTAL TIME 10 MINUTES

Mum used to make this for breakfast or pack it up as a roti parcel for us to take to school. I loved it, but it was so different to the eggs I was seeing on TV: delicate, soft scrambled and poached with hollandaise. Mum's eggs were overcooked and chewy. They broke all the rules of Western egg cooking. But now that I'm older, I know about all kinds of different eggs: American scramble, high-heat fried eggs with crispy edges, curries with browned boiled eggs. Mum's eggs weren't overcooked, they were perfectly cooked for the dish. The Maillard reaction (page 13) gives them a deep savoury flavour, and the extra time gives a meaty chew. They're not delicate, but they're just as good.

3 eggs
¼ cup (60 ml) light olive oil
½ brown onion, roughly
    chopped
1 bird's eye chilli, roughly
    chopped
Pinch of cumin seeds
2–3 sprigs fresh coriander
    (cilantro), leaves picked,
    plus extra to serve
Fresh or frozen roti (for fresh,
    page 57) or toast

Crack the eggs into a bowl, add a pinch of salt and whisk until uniform. Heat the oil in a frying pan over medium–high heat, then add the onion, chilli and cumin seeds. Cook until the onion is golden brown, about 3–4 minutes. Add the egg mixture and coriander, then mix, stirring periodically, to get a chunky scramble. Cook until you have a slight golden colour on the eggs, 2–3 minutes.

If serving with roti, heat them up (if fresh, see page 57, or per packet instructions). Place the eggs on the roti, sprinkle with extra coriander and wrap up or serve with toast.

Fried School Prawns

SERVES 4–6 × ACTIVE TIME 15 MINUTES × TOTAL TIME 25 MINUTES

If you've never had school prawns, imagine your favourite prawn, shot with a shrink ray to the size of a 20-cent coin. Still a prawn, just miniature. Get those tiny prawns, dredge them in flour and spices, then deep-fry them whole — head, shell, legs, everything — getting all the flavour of the prawn in there. It's crispy, but it still has a bit of chew from the meat. It's like prawn popcorn, so satisfying and so addictive. I'm salivating just thinking about it.

1 tablespoon white vinegar
500 g (1 lb 2 oz) baby school
    prawns (shrimp)
Neutral high smoke point oil,
    for deep-frying
1 tablespoon fine rice flour or
    plain (all-purpose) flour

SEASONING
1 teaspoon Fiji masala powder
    or garam masala
1 teaspoon ground turmeric
½ teaspoon ground cumin
½ teaspoon chilli powder
½ teaspoon salt, or to taste

TO SERVE
Fried curry leaves (optional)
Chilli Chutney (page 218)
Beer (optional)
Rice (page 28) and Dhal
    (page 80, both optional)

Combine the vinegar and 2 cups (500 ml) water in a bowl. Wash the prawns in the vinegar mixture, drain and pat dry with paper towel. Cut off their antennas (using scissors is the easiest method).

Heat the oil in a cast iron frying pan over medium heat or a deep fryer to 170–180°C (340–360°F). (If you don't have a probe, put a wooden spoon in the oil. If small bubbles appear around the spoon, it's ready.) Line a plate with paper towel.

Meanwhile, mix the seasoning in a bowl, then transfer half to a separate bowl and reserve for later. Mix the flour into the other bowl of seasoning, then add the prawns. Mix until the prawns are coated.

In batches, deep-fry the prawns until GBD (see page 13), about 2–5 minutes. Drain the prawns on the paper towel-lined plate.

When you've fried all the prawns (they should still be warm), put them in a clean bowl and sprinkle over the reserved seasoning while mixing constantly. Sprinkle with fried curry leaves, if using.

Serve with chilli chutney, beer (not a big beer guy but it feels right) as a little snack or with rice and dhal.

TIP You can sub the prawns out for whitebait, it's the same timing. You're just looking for golden brown from the deep-fry.

Indian Smoked Eggplant (Baigan Choka)

SERVES 4 × ACTIVE TIME 25 MINUTES × TOTAL TIME 35 MINUTES

Baigan choka is a smoked eggplant dish like baba ganoush. It's my favourite way to enjoy eggplant: smoky and creamy, but with texture and freshness from onion and fresh coriander.

This is an adapted recipe. In Fiji, it would be cooked on an outdoor stove over fire and left to smoke. We used to do the same thing with a barbecue after we'd finished cooking our meat. Mum would just say, 'Put an eggplant on and we'll have baigan choka tomorrow.' We'd just leave it over the embers. This version uses a stove, barbecue or oven to make it easy.

1 large eggplant (aubergine)
2 garlic cloves, halved
½ red onion, finely chopped
1 bird's eye chilli, finely
    chopped
Small handful of fresh
    coriander (cilantro) leaves,
    finely chopped
2 teaspoons lemon juice
    (from about ¼ lemon)

TO SERVE
Roti (page 57) or Rice
    (page 28)

Use a knife to make 4 slits in the eggplant, then stuff with the garlic halves.

OPTION 1: STOVE OR BARBECUE
Place the eggplant on a wire rack over a gas stove or on a barbecue grill plate on high or over coals. Allow it to char on one section, then turn and char the next section. Repeat until it's charred all over – this will take about 10–15 minutes. Transfer to a bowl, cover it with plastic wrap and let it steam until completely soft and cooked through, about 10 minutes.

OPTION 2: OVEN
Preheat the oven to 220°C (430°F). Dry roast the eggplant for 15–20 minutes, then remove from the oven and transfer to a bowl. Cover with plastic wrap and let it steam until completely soft and cooked through, 5–10 minutes.

Unwrap the eggplant, peel and discard the skin. Place it in a clean bowl and mash with a fork, ensuring you mash the garlic as well. Add the onion, chilli, coriander and lemon juice. Season with salt and mix. Taste and adjust with salt according to taste.

Serve at room temperature with roti or rice.

Fiji Fish

I feel like every ethnic person has smuggled some sort of fresh fruit, vegetable or piece of meat from their country of origin into Australia. It happens all the time. Every time we came back from Fiji, we would bring turmeric, Fiji masala, kava and seafood. Apparently, it's legal. One thing we'd always get is frozen fish. Mum would have them cleaned, cut, vacuum packed and labelled – that's probably what made it legal. Mum and Dad called it Fiji fish, but I was always thinking, what the heck is it?

Me: Mum, what type of fish is this?

Mum: Fiji Fish.

Me: What do you mean?

Mum: It's the fish you get from Fiji.

Me: Yeah, but what type of fish is it?

Mum: Fiji Fish.

Me: Mum, that's not a type of fish. What breed is it?

Mum: It's just Fiji fish.

That's how it was growing up. I had no idea. When I went back to Fiji, I found out it wasn't just one fish. It could be mahi-mahi, walu, Spanish mackerel, sometimes even rock cod. They're all Fiji fish. They would either make a curry or wash the fish in lemon juice, cut it into chunks, cover it with spices and deep-fry it.

Fiji Fry Fish (Machli Fry)

SERVES 4-6 × ACTIVE/TOTAL TIME 30 MINUTES + 1 HOUR MARINATING

1 kg (2 lb 4 oz) whole King George whiting or 1 kg (2 lb 4 oz) Spanish mackerel cutlets, 3—4 cm (1¼—1½ inch) thick, cut into quarters
1 tablespoon lemon juice (from about ½ lemon)
¾ teaspoon ground turmeric
2 teaspoons ground coriander
½ teaspoon chilli powder
1 teaspoon ground cumin
½ teaspoon salt
2 tablespoons fine rice flour or plain (all-purpose) flour
Neutral high smoke point oil, for deep-frying
Flaky sea salt, to season

TO SERVE
Curry leaves
Dhal (page 80) and Rice (page 28, both optional)

Gut the whole fish and clean well (a fishmonger will usually do this for you). Pat the fish or fish pieces dry with paper towel and place in a bowl. Coat in the lemon juice, then add all the spices and salt. Gently toss the fish until evenly coated. Sprinkle with the flour and toss again, then cover with plastic wrap and place in the fridge for 1 hour to marinate.

Not long before the fish comes out of the fridge, heat the oil in a cast iron frying pan over medium heat or a deep fryer to 170—180°C (340—360°F). (If you don't have a probe, put a wooden spoon in the oil. If small bubbles appear around the spoon, it's ready.) Line a plate with paper towel.

Deep-fry (you can use the same oil for the fish after) the curry leaves until crispy — when the crackle stops, about 15 seconds. Drain on the paper towel-lined plate.

Deep-fry the fish for around 2 minutes on one side, then turn and fry for another 2—3 minutes on the other side — they should be golden and crunchy. Drain on the paper towel-lined plate and while still hot, hit them with a pinch of flaky sea salt.

Garnish with the fried curry leaves and serve with dhal and rice or enjoy it as a snack on its own.

As pictured on page 43

Rosella Leaf Chutney (Khatta Bhaji)

SERVES 4-8 × ACTIVE TIME 25 MINUTES × TOTAL TIME 35 MINUTES

This is ugly, but it's the kind of dish — one that may never be pretty enough to be served in a fancy restaurant — that I'll always love the most. It's halfway between a condiment and a curry. The flavour is very concentrated. It's this intensely sour, spicy, garlicky, creamy chutney with a spinach-like texture. Eat it with a combination of curries or spread a thin amount of it on a roti like any other condiment. I don't know if it was illegal, but my nani (maternal grandma) in Fiji would make it, wrap it up in a roti and smuggle it from Fiji to Australia. Either that or she'd cook it, freeze it and bring it with her on the plane.

4 small eggplants (aubergines)
⅓ cup (80 ml) vegetable oil
½ small brown onion,
    finely chopped
½ head of garlic, cloves
    roughly chopped
6 bird's eye chillies, halved
    lengthways
1 teaspoon cumin seeds
40 fresh curry leaves (from
    about 3 sprigs), roughly
    chopped
260 g (9¼ oz) rosella leaves
    (fresh is best, but we
    used frozen)

TO SERVE
Roti (page 57) or Dhal (page
    80) and Rice (page 28)

Roughly dice the eggplants and put them in a bowl of water (to prevent browning/oxidising).

Heat the oil in a saucepan, then add the onion, garlic and chilli. Cook until the onion is translucent, about 3–5 minutes. Add the cumin and curry leaves. Cook for another 1–2 minutes, then add the eggplant, rosella leaves and a pinch of salt. Cover and cook over low heat until everything has softened, about 10–15 minutes.

Mash in the pan using a wooden pestle or potato masher — this takes a good 10 minutes (see tip). Taste and season with salt.

Serve wrapped up in some roti or with dhal and rice.

TIP It might be tempting to blend instead of mashing, but you won't get the right texture. It'll be sticky and gummy. You need to mash it in the pan. It takes like 10 minutes — a lot of effort, but it will keep Nani happy.

Raita

SERVES 4–6 × ACTIVE/TOTAL TIME 10 MINUTES

Usually my family would have raita as an accompaniment to a couple of curries or Mum's palau. As I learned about other cuisines, I got introduced to tzatziki and it reminded me so much of raita – please don't get offended. I don't know if raita is the Indian tzatziki or if tzatziki is the Greek raita, but making the comparison really opened up my mind about how I could use raita. Now, I have it as a standalone dish, with crackers, on veggies or in a sandwich.

Here are two versions, the classic that we'd use as a condiment for curries, and a heartier, chunky version you can serve as a side or salad (it's great with the Roast Chicken Curry on page 91 or Masala Roast Spanish Mackerel on page 188).

CLASSIC RAITA
1 Lebanese (short) cucumber
½ small carrot
1 cup (260 g) Greek-style
   yoghurt
½ red onion, finely chopped
½ bird's eye chilli, finely
   chopped
1 small bunch of fresh
   coriander (cilantro), leaves
   picked and finely chopped
1 teaspoon ground cumin
   (see tip)

Using the coarse side of a box grater, grate the cucumber and carrot. Using your hands, squeeze out as much of the moisture as you can (you could squeeze it into a glass and shot it – I'm sure it's good for you). Place in a bowl with the yoghurt, onion, chilli, coriander and cumin. Taste, adjust with salt and serve.

CHUNKY CUCUMBER RAITA 'SALAD'
3 Lebanese (short) cucumbers
1 cup (260 g) Greek-style
   yoghurt
1 long green chilli, thinly sliced
1 garlic clove, crushed
1 small bunch of fresh
   coriander (cilantro), leaves
   picked and finely chopped
1 teaspoon ground cumin
   (see tip)

TO SERVE
Pickled red onion or very thinly
   sliced red onion

Cut the cucumbers into random chunks and place them in a bowl. Mix in all the remaining ingredients and season with salt to taste. Garnish with pickled or fresh red onion.

TIP What makes a good raita is toasting and grinding your own cumin seeds. That's a rule for making the most of spices generally, but it makes a huge difference in raita. That's my secret.

My favourite dessert

I have a favourite dessert for different meals, but growing up, payasam was always the one.

It's really hard to describe. When I was working on this book, these are all the ways I tried to describe it:

1. It's like a very runny porridge.

2. Think of it like a bubble tea, but as a soup.

3. It's kind of like a dessert soup.

4. Imagine a milky, sweet drink in a paper cup.

5. An overly milky sago pudding flavoured with cardamom.

See, it's so hard. None of them sound appetising, but it's delicious. My friends all love it or hate it (probably because of the texture), but the ones who hate it need to learn how to live.

When I was growing up, my mum was the designated payasam maker at weddings and big family events. Mum and the other women would ladle it into paper cups from a massive pot. As kids, our job was to go around with a tray of cups and hand it out to all the guests. Once we were done and everyone was letting loose and partying, I would be chilling wherever the food was, sipping on payasam.

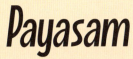

Payasam

SERVES 10–12 × ACTIVE TIME 15 MINUTES × TOTAL TIME 1 HOUR 15 MINUTES

½ cup (100 g) moong dhal (find at selected supermarkets)

1 tablespoon ghee, plus extra for frying

¼ cup (45 g) small sago (find at selected supermarkets)

¼ cup (40 g) roasted vermicelli (find at selected supermarkets)

340 ml (11½ fl oz) can evaporated milk

395 g (13¾ oz) can sweetened condensed milk

2 tablespoons roughly chopped pistachio kernels

2 tablespoons slivered almonds

2 teaspoons vanilla essence or 1 vanilla pod

½ teaspoon ground cardamom

¼ fresh nutmeg, finely grated

Wash the moong dhal thoroughly. Heat the ghee in a saucepan over medium heat, then add the moong dhal and a pinch of salt. Cook for 5 minutes. Pour in 1½ cups (375 ml) water and bring to the boil. Cook until the moong dhal becomes soft, about 30–45 minutes. While it's boiling, place the sago and vermicelli in two separate bowls, cover each with water and allow to soak for 30 minutes.

Once the moong dhal is soft, drain the sago, add to the pan and cook with the moong dhal for 2 minutes. Drain the vermicelli, add to the pan and cook for another 2 minutes. Pour in the evaporated milk and three-quarters of the condensed milk, stir and taste for sweetness. (Add the remaining condensed milk if you like it sweeter.) Keep the heat on low.

Meanwhile, heat a little extra ghee in a small frying pan over medium heat, then add the pistachios and almonds and toast until the nuts start to turn golden brown, about 2–3 minutes.

Add the nuts to the saucepan. Place the vanilla, cardamom and nutmeg in a small bowl, then slowly pour in a little water until a paste forms. Add the paste to the saucepan (the water will prevent lumps), simmer for 5 minutes, then cut the heat.

If you want it hot, serve. If you want it cold, chuck it in the fridge and take it out once it's cool and serve.

TIP If you need to make a bulk dessert, this is so easy. You also don't need to put vermicelli in it. I included it in this recipe because Mum always does.

Non-Traditional Kokoda

SERVES 4 × ACTIVE TIME 15 MINUTES × TOTAL TIME 25 MINUTES

Kokoda is a traditional Fijian dish, but I didn't grow up eating it. I learned about it when I was getting more into Fijian cuisine and culture. Traditionally, it's raw fish cured in lime until completely cooked through and served in a coconut shell with fresh coconut cream, diced cucumber, capsicum (pepper), onion, chilli and coriander. You could say it's like ceviche or crudo, but I want it to stand on its own — I hope one day it might be as famous as those dishes. This is my spin on it, which uses a shorter curing time for more texture and adds in chilli chutney, which is a killer pairing.

200–300 g (7–10½ oz)
 sashimi-grade fish
 (see tips)
1 French shallot
1 garlic clove
70–80 ml (2¼–2½ fl oz)
 lime juice (from about
 4–5 limes)
100 ml (3½ fl oz) coconut
 cream
1 teaspoon Chilli Chutney
 (page 218)
2 tablespoons extra virgin
 olive oil
2 baby cucumbers,
 finely chopped
¼ bunch of fresh coriander
 (cilantro), stems
 finely chopped

Pat dry the fish with paper towel, cut into 1 cm (½ inch) thick slices and place in a bowl. Blend the shallot, garlic, 70 ml (2¼ fl oz) lime juice and a pinch of salt in a blender until smooth. Strain the blended liquid over the fish. If the mixture isn't mostly covering the fish, add some more of the lime juice. Allow the fish to cure in the liquid for 5–10 minutes in the fridge.

Once it's done, set aside 2 tablespoons of the curing liquid and drain the fish well. Add the reserved curing liquid to a bowl or jug, mix in the coconut cream and season to taste. In a separate bowl, mix the chutney and oil, then set aside. In yet another bowl, mix the cucumber and coriander stems (you want the cucumber and coriander stems to be roughly equal in volume) to form a little salad.

To assemble, place the fish on a serving plate, sprinkle with the cucumber and coriander salad, drizzle the coconut dressing and the chilli chutney oil over the top, Jackson Pollock style, and serve immediately.

TIPS If you find a whole sashimi-grade fish (600–700 g/1 lb 5 oz–1 lb 9 oz), plating up the whole fish with the kokoda on top looks amazing. Simply fillet the fish, slice into 1 cm (½ inch) pieces and cure. Then drain and place back onto the fish carcass. Double the recipe of the coconut dressing and chilli chutney oil and drizzle on top.

If you're at the fishmonger, ask them what sashimi-grade fish they have. They may have quite a few options. My preference is snapper. I like the texture and flavour. It's a bit more delicate and sweet. Kingfish is a classic and can also be much easier to find as a sashimi-grade fish.

(Lolo Buns) # Coconut Buns

MAKES 6 × ACTIVE TIME 30 MINUTES × TOTAL TIME 60 MINUTES + 2½–3½ HOURS PROOFING

Lolo buns are a traditional Fijian bread. Imagine the lightest, most pillowy dinner roll, then cover it in coconut cream. The bottom of it is custardy and dense, and the top is light and caramelised. It's both sweet and savoury. It's really interesting.

This isn't a traditional recipe I had growing up though. The only lolo buns I've eaten are the ones I've made. Making them was part of me trying to discover Fijian food. I wanted to know more about what the cuisine is. I did some research into the buns and invited my parents to come over. I made Roast Chicken Curry (page 91), some fennel experiment and lolo buns. The fennel was crap, but the curry and the lolo buns were bangers.

240 g (8½ oz) plain (all-purpose) flour
85 g (3 oz) plain wholemeal flour
45 g (1½ oz) caster (superfine) sugar
5 g (⅛ oz) salt
4 g (⅛ oz) active dry yeast
55 g (2 oz) unsalted butter, melted
1 cup (250 ml) milk
200 ml (7 fl oz) coconut cream

Mix all the dry ingredients in a large bowl. Add the melted butter and milk to the mixture and mix until combined, then knead the dough on a clean work surface until smooth and it bounces back, about 10 minutes. Place the dough in a lightly greased bowl, cover with plastic wrap and allow to rest for 1½ hours in a warm/room-temperature environment.

Preheat the oven to 180°C (360°F).

To deflate the dough, make a fist and give it a punch (it feels therapeutic), then separate it into six equal balls. Place each ball, evenly spaced, on a baking tray or in a cast iron frying pan, cover with a damp tea (dish) towel or plastic wrap and rest until the dough has doubled in size, about 1–2 hours.

Pour the coconut cream over the dough, making sure to divide it equally between each dough ball. Bake until deeply GBD (see page 13), around 25–30 minutes.

Fiji Milk Ice Blocks

MAKES 10–12 × ACTIVE/TOTAL TIME 15 MINUTES + OVERNIGHT FREEZING

Every suburb in Fiji has a corner shop with these milk ice blocks. When I was a kid, they were the best thing ever. I always got the pink one, I don't know why. I'm pretty sure they were all the same flavour, but it was the best. When I went to Fiji with my wife Esther for the first time and we were on the way to the airport to go home, I realised she hadn't had a Fiji ice block yet. I made a special detour to make sure she tried one. She'd never had anything like it, she loved it. That didn't matter though, I was just happy to share a childhood memory with her.

I did six recipes before I figured out how to make this. It was so annoying. Just testing, looking online, trial and error. This is the closest I could get to what I remember.

4 cups (1 litre) milk (see tip)
130 g (4½ oz) milk powder
240 g (8½ oz) caster
  (superfine) sugar
340 ml (11½ fl oz) can
  evaporated milk
395 g (13¾ oz) can sweetened
  condensed milk
½ teaspoon vanilla essence
3–4 drops food colouring
  (optional, your choice but
  pink is classic)

Place all the ingredients, except the food colouring, in a saucepan and bring to a simmer. Simmer, stirring constantly, until the sugar and milk powder dissolve, about 5 minutes. Pour the mixture into a bowl and allow it to cool down to room temperature.

Add the food colouring, if you want. Mix and pour into ice block moulds or plastic cups. Insert sticks and carefully place them in the freezer overnight.

TIP Get Jersey milk — it's fattier than regular milk and makes the ice block much creamier.

Yoghurt Rice (Dahi Bhat)

Tata (Grandpa) was always in the garden. Whenever it was a hot day, he would always ask Parti (Grandma) to make dahi bhat, which is just yoghurt and rice. Even if she had already cooked all these other things, he would still want to eat dahi bhat.

To the rice and yoghurt, he would add thinly sliced onions, salt and pickled chillies on the side. He'd mash the rice, yoghurt and salt together with his hands, have a bit of it, then take a bite of pickled chillies, then another bite with the yoghurt and so on. Even though I was probably ten at the time, I would be sitting with Tata trying to keep up with the amount of chillies he ate. It's poor man's food — you'd never serve this to guests — but it didn't matter if we were doing well or not, Tata loved it.

Whenever I see yoghurt and rice, I instantly think of my grandpa. It's crazy how powerful food can be, just one look and I'm instantly in the garden of my childhood house with him, eating pickled chillies.

Everyone has one of those dishes, and I think talking about them and sharing them is important. Food is all just ingredients, and sometimes it takes hours or even days to bring those ingredients together. Sometimes it takes just a minute. It doesn't matter if it's caviar and wagyu at a fancy restaurant or yoghurt and rice in your backyard. What matters is that you made someone feel something.

There are no quantities for a recipe like this; you have to do it by feel. I go by ratio: one part yoghurt to two parts rice. Put in as little or as much onion as you want.

Yoghurt
Cooked rice
Red onion, sliced as thin
    as possible
Pickled Chillies (page 228)

Just put everything, except the chillies, together on a plate and mix it with your hands. Serve with the chillies on the side. Eat with your hands and take a bite of the chillies every now and then.

Roti

MAKES 10–12 × ACTIVE TIME 25 MINUTES × TOTAL TIME 30 MINUTES

This is the bread my family would have with every meal. It's so labour-intensive, but Mum would always make it fresh. She does it so quickly. She can bang out 20–30 rotis from scratch in 20 minutes, easily. She would be cooking a roti and rolling a new roti at the same time, and every single one would be perfectly round. She makes it look so easy, but that's very, very hard to do. There's this joke in Indian culture, to be a good wife you need to roll a perfectly round roti. Unsurprisingly, I'd make a horrible wife.

This is a recipe where you need to feel it out. The texture you're looking for after kneading it is playdough. Trust the process, it will come together. Just keep going.

2 teaspoons (10 g) honey
2 cups (300 g) atta flour, plus
    extra if needed (see tip)
2 tablespoons olive oil

TO SERVE
Your favourite curry

Boil a saucepan or kettle of at least 1½ cups (375 ml) water. Take off the heat and let the water cool down for 5 minutes, then mix the honey into 1½ cups (375 ml) of the water until dissolved. (I've measured the temperature my mum uses, it's about 90°C/195°F.)

Place the flour and about 1 tablespoon oil in a bowl and mix with your hands, then slowly add the honey water. Mix with a fork (it's too hot to use your hands) until it's a dry, shaggy mess. At this point, it should be cool enough to use your hands, so work it into a dough. Knead on a clean work surface for a few minutes until the dough is looking smooth. Add the remaining oil and knead some more until you have a soft, smooth and playdough-like dough, about 5–10 minutes all up. Make adjustments with extra flour or hot water if you need to.

Cover the dough with a damp tea (dish) towel and rest in a warm environment for 5 minutes, then divide into large golf ball-sized balls. Dust the work surface or cutting board with extra flour (this will prevent the dough from sticking) and roll each ball out until it's 1–2 mm (1⁄16 inch) thick.

Heat a frying pan over medium–high heat, then cook one roti for 20–30 seconds on one side, then flip and cook for 30–45 seconds on the other side. Do a final third flip and cook for another 30 seconds. On the third flip, you should be looking for a bit of browning and some puffing up (you don't want it to go black, so adjust the heat if it's too hot or not hot enough). When it's done, set aside under a clean tea towel. If you have a roti or tortilla warmer, use that. Repeat with the remaining roti, adding each following roti to the stack and covering with the tea towel. When you're finished, serve with your favourite curry.

TIP You can get atta flour at your local Indian grocer. If you can't do that, an alternative is a 50/50 mix of wholemeal and plain (all-purpose) flour.

'In my heart, I am Indian but my food is Fijian-Indian. It's a mix of foods. We have embraced Fijian culture and they have embraced ours. In India it's different; the spices are heavy. Fijian-Indian food is very mild and simple. I love to cook for my family. I hope people try my recipes and I hope they enjoy it.'

— Justin's Mum

As a kid, I remember watching Indian cooks. When they cooked a dish, they'd have a name for it. Even just for chicken curries — there's jalfrezi-style chicken curry with fresh tomatoes, there's a hariyali chicken curry with yoghurt at the base and so many other variants. But in my family, it was always just murgi tarkari, the Fiji Hindi words for chicken curry.

When I researched the history of Fijian-Indian culture, it was a mess. In the 1800s when the British colonised the world (thanks for that), they took a whole bunch of Indians all over the place. A lot ended up in Fiji, working in the sugar fields as indentured labourers. There were people from all over India in those fields. For generations, you had people from the north, central and south of India marrying each other on these small islands. Families were sharing language and recipes in this new environment and some things got lost in translation. Over time the nuances of their food and culture changed. My family has a Tamil background in South India, but they don't speak Tamil; they speak a mix of Hindi and Urdu because that's what was spoken in Fiji. Parti's (Grandma's) cooking was the same; it was South Indian but it had all these other techniques from different parts of India. She used dairy and coconut, sometimes at the same time. She could only use what she had access to and that included taro and other local ingredients, as well as soy sauce from the Chinese influence there. Fiji took the culture and cuisine from India and made it their own.

This was the food I grew up with, Parti and Mum's rogue and resourceful Fijian version of Indian food. Of course, they never wrote any of it down (that's a Western tradition, the Indian way of learning is to go into a kitchen and watch someone cook). The curries in this chapter are my attempt (and I think it's a pretty good attempt) to translate their home cooking. But, like my grandma, use whatever is in your pantry or growing in your garden, change whatever you like and feel free to make it up. You've got my permission. The main rule is there are no rules.

How to Make a Good Curry

WHAT FAT OR OIL TO USE

In Fiji, Mum used a seed or coconut oil, but when she came to Australia she started using olive oil. I've done tests with ghee, light olive oil and neutral oils. There isn't a massive difference between olive oil and neutral oils, but with ghee you do notice it's fattier and richer, which I don't always like. The nostalgic oil for me is olive oil, so I use that.

HOW MUCH HEAT TO USE

I've put medium heat on most of the curry recipes, but traditionally most start with high heat to brown the onion, then lower to add the garlic and powdered spices. But to do that you need to have your prep done and organised, so you can move quickly. If you're confident, smash the heat from the beginning.

TEMPERING

Tempering is simply cooking spices, onion and other aromats in oil. It's the most pivotal part of getting flavour into a curry. Cooking spices in fat opens them up and releases their flavour and aroma. Technically, what you're doing is infusing the oil; making a flavoured oil that will perfume and infuse the whole dish with flavour.

Make sure you use a good amount of oil. You will know when the spices are ready, because the aroma will hit you. It's the same for powdered and whole spices, but powdered spices don't take as long — you'll see most recipes add them later on. Be careful with powdered spices, because if they burn, they can be bitter and acrid.

ONIONS AND GARLIC

After tempering, the most important part of making a good curry is browning the onion — it adds depth, sweetness and savouriness. You're looking for translucent onion with a thin bit of golden brown — go a little lighter on for veg curries and full golden brown for meat curries. A bit of char doesn't hurt; as long as it's not black and burnt, you're fine. Garlic is different. Make sure you don't burn it — a light golden brown is okay, but you don't want to go further or it can give you a bitter, acrid taste.

SPICES

You can buy spices in bulk at Indian grocers way cheaper than at the supermarket. If you want a next-level flavour, get whole spices, toast them at home, then grind them. Also, remember spices (like all ingredients) vary. Your turmeric and the turmeric I use might be different in flavour. Same with chilli and any other ingredient. Always taste and make adjustments that work for you.

GINGER AND GARLIC PASTES

Because I'm making so many recipes that require garlic and ginger, I keep jars of garlic and ginger paste in my fridge. I make my own in bulk. Get a whole heap of garlic and ginger, peel, roughly chop and blend each separately with a pinch of salt and a little oil (to help extend the shelf life), then place each in a clean jar and store in the fridge. For 1 cup (about 150 g) chopped garlic or ginger, go with a pinch of salt (2–4 g/⅛ oz) and 1–2 tablespoons oil. If you can't be bothered, buy some, but I find the flavour of store-bought to be more subdued, so you may need to add more to the recipe to get the same impact as fresh garlic/ginger or a homemade paste.

The Mixture

When I was in Perth, wanting to learn about Indian food, I'd call my mum.

Me: Mum, what do you put in this curry?

Mum: Turmeric and mixture.

Me: What mixture?

Mum: You know, the mixture.

Me: Mum, you use a thousand different spices. I don't know what the mixture is.

We had so many funny conversations like that. Eventually, I found out it's a combination of cumin seeds, black mustard seeds and fenugreek seeds. We use it in almost all our curries. You'll see a lot of the recipes in this book have those three whole spices in the same ratio. If you're going to cook a lot of curries, it'll be easier if you have a jar of this ready to go. Keep in an airtight container for up to a year.

2 tablespoons cumin seeds
2 tablespoons black mustard seeds
1 tablespoon fenugreek seeds

Combine all the ingredients in a jar. If you want a bigger quantity, use the same ratio of cumin, mustard and fenugreek seeds (2:2:1).

Fiji Crab Curry (Kekada Tarkari)

SERVES 6–8 × ACTIVE TIME 25 MINUTES × TOTAL TIME 35 MINUTES

Never wear a white T-shirt to crab curry night. It's a mess. Everyone is all around the table, hands dirty, just getting in there. You can hear cracking, sucking, crab juice getting squirted into people's eyes, the sound of people blowing their nose from all the spice (Mum goes hard on chilli for crab) and everyone passing the crab claws they can't crack to Mum (I don't know what the PSI of Mum's jaw is, but she just crunches into it). Then, when everyone has their crabmeat, there is silence as the meal is devoured.

1 kg (2 lb 4 oz) mud crabs
    (about 2 mud crabs)
25 g (1 oz) fresh tamarind
    soaked in 100 ml (3½ fl oz)
    warm water (see tip) or
    1 tablespoon store-bought
    tamarind paste
½ cup (125 ml) light olive oil
1 large brown onion, finely
    chopped
1 sprig fresh curry leaves
1 teaspoon The Mixture
    (opposite page) or
    ¼ teaspoon each of
    cumin seeds and black
    mustard seeds, and
    ⅛ teaspoon fenugreek seeds
10–12 garlic cloves, crushed,
    or 2 tablespoons garlic
    paste (page 59)
10 g (¼ oz) fresh ginger,
    finely grated, or
    1 teaspoon ginger
    paste (page 59)
1 tablespoon ground turmeric
1 teaspoon chilli powder
2 tablespoons Fijian masala
    powder
1 large tomato, finely chopped
2 cups (500 ml) hot water
200 ml (7 fl oz) coconut cream

TO SERVE
¼ bunch of fresh coriander
    (cilantro), leaves and stems
    roughly chopped
Roti (page 57) and Rice
    (page 28)

Prepare the crabs by washing thoroughly. To break apart, twist the claws off the body, then remove the top shell from the body and discard it along with the gills (aka dead man's fingers). Break or cut the body into four roughly equal parts. With the back of a cleaver, rolling pin or pestle, crack the claws (just enough for a hairline fracture). If this is confusing, just watch a YouTube video. Place the claws and all body parts in a large bowl, cover with the tamarind paste and mix. Set aside.

Heat the oil in a large saucepan over high heat, then add the onion, curry leaves and whole spices and cook until the onion is golden brown, about 3–5 minutes. Add the garlic, ginger, turmeric, chilli and masala powders and season with salt (I do about 1 teaspoon). Mix well. Add the tomato. Cook until the tomato breaks down and you have an almost paste-like consistency, about 5 minutes. Add the crab and mix well. Pour in the hot water, bring to a simmer and cook until the liquid has reduced by about one-third and the crab shells turn orange, about 10 minutes.

Mix in the coconut cream, taste and adjust with salt. Let it cook for 5 more minutes.

Garnish with the coriander. Serve with roti and rice.

TIP You can use store-bought tamarind paste in a jar or make your own with fresh tamarind. I find the jar tamarind is quite sharp and acidic. Fresh tamarind is more earthy, nuanced and has a deeper flavour. Make your own by soaking tamarind pods (find at your local Asian grocer or specialty grocer) in warm water until just covered for 30 minutes, then use your hands to separate the flesh from the seeds and fibrous bits (the flesh and water will form a paste). If you don't have tamarind, you can add a squeeze of lemon to finish the curry.

As pictured on pages 62–63 | **EVERYTHING IS INDIAN**

Fiji Crab Curry
(page 61)

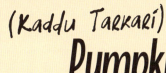

(Kaddu Tarkari)
Pumpkin Tamarind Curry

SERVES 4-6 × ACTIVE TIME 20 MINUTES × TOTAL TIME 30 MINUTES

This may be my favourite way to eat pumpkin. Growing up, there were two ways to make this curry: with or without tamarind. Tamarind, which adds sourness, is Parti's (Grandma's) version, so of course, I liked that one, but you can go without if you want a classic pumpkin curry. I use Kent pumpkin (squash), but just use what you have if you have a pumpkin already.

¼ cup (60 ml) light olive oil
½ brown onion, finely chopped
1–2 bird's eye chillies,
    halved lengthways
1 sprig fresh curry leaves
1 teaspoon The Mixture
    (page 60) or ¼ teaspoon
    each of cumin seeds and
    black mustard seeds, and
    ⅛ teaspoon fenugreek seeds
8–9 garlic cloves, crushed,
    or 1¼ tablespoons garlic
    paste (page 59)
10 g (¼ oz) fresh ginger,
    finely grated, or
    1 teaspoon ginger
    paste (page 59)
1 teaspoon ground turmeric
1 teaspoon ground cumin
800 g (1 lb 12 oz, about
    ½ small–medium) Kent
    or butternut pumpkin
    (squash), sliced into
    1–2 cm (½–¾ inch) cubes,
    skin on or off, up to you
5 g (⅛ oz) fresh tamarind
    soaked in 2 tablespoons
    warm water for 30 minutes
    (see tip, page 61) or
    2 teaspoons store-bought
    tamarind paste
10 g (¼ oz) unsalted butter

TO SERVE
1 bunch of fresh coriander
    (cilantro), leaves and stems
    roughly chopped
Roti (page 57), Rice (page 28)
    and a few other curries

Heat the oil in a large saucepan over medium heat, then add the onion, chilli, curry leaves and whole spices and cook until the onion turns golden brown, about 3–5 minutes. Add the garlic and ginger and cook for another minute. Stir in the turmeric, cumin and a pinch of salt. Add the pumpkin and mix all the ingredients. Cover with a lid and let it cook, stirring every 5 or so minutes to prevent sticking, until the pumpkin is soft, about 20–25 minutes.

If using fresh tamarind, discard the seeds and pod (the liquid and flesh will become a paste). Mix this tamarind paste and the butter into the curry. Taste and adjust with salt.

Top with the coriander and serve as part of a spread with roti, rice and other curries.

Egg Curry

(Anda Tarkari)

SERVES 4–6 × ACTIVE TIME 20 MINUTES × TOTAL TIME 30 MINUTES

This was always on regular rotation in our household, but mainly just for family. For guests, Mum would usually do a lamb, chicken or something that seemed a little more 'premium'. Now, egg curry is one of my go-tos and, honestly, I cook it when I'm trying to be cheap. When I have guests coming over, I want to give them a unique, delicious experience and show them who I am. Egg curry is part of that.

6 eggs, at room temperature
¼–⅓ cup (60–80 ml) light
    olive oil
1 large brown onion,
    thinly sliced
15–20 fresh curry leaves
2 bird's eye chillies, halved
    lengthways
1 teaspoon The Mixture
    (page 60) or ¼ teaspoon
    each of cumin seeds and
    black mustard seeds, and
    ⅛ teaspoon fenugreek seeds
½ teaspoon ground turmeric
½ teaspoon ground cumin
¼ teaspoon chilli powder
4 garlic cloves, crushed,
    or 1 tablespoon garlic
    paste (page 59)
1 large ripe tomato, roughly
    diced or ½ × 400 g (14 oz)
    can diced tomatoes
    (see tip)

TO SERVE
¼ bunch of fresh coriander
    (cilantro), leaves and stems
    roughly chopped
Roti (page 57) and Rice
    (page 28)

Pour some iced water into a bowl. Bring a saucepan of water to a gentle boil, then add the eggs. Boil for 6 minutes, then immediately transfer them to the iced water. Once cool enough to handle, peel the eggs.

Line a plate with paper towel. Heat the oil in a frying pan over medium heat. Fry the boiled eggs until golden brown all over, about 1–2 minutes. Drain the eggs on the paper-towel lined plate.

In the same pan, add the onion, curry leaves, fresh chilli and whole spices and cook until the onion is golden brown, about 3–4 minutes. Add the powdered spices and a pinch of salt and mix. Add the garlic and tomato and cook until the tomato has completely broken down, about 5–6 minutes. Return the eggs to the pan and simmer for 2–5 minutes so all the ingredients get to know each other.

Taste and adjust with salt. Garnish with the coriander and serve with roti and rice.

TIP If you don't have fresh tomato, use half a can of tomatoes and you'll get the same result. Use the whole tin if you want it to be saucier.

As pictured on pages 68–69

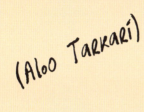 

(Aloo Tarkari) Potato Curry

SERVES 4–6 × ACTIVE TIME 30 MINUTES × TOTAL TIME 40 MINUTES

While other families were eating mashed potato, we were eating potato curry. It was a dinner table staple and one of two things Mum put in the roti parcels she made for us to take to school. Indian scrambled eggs was the other.

5 potatoes
3 tablespoons light olive oil
½ brown onion, finely chopped
1 bird's eye chilli, halved
    lengthways
15–20 fresh curry leaves
1 teaspoon The Mixture
    (page 60) or ¼ teaspoon
    each of cumin seeds and
    black mustard seeds, and
    ⅛ teaspoon fenugreek seeds
3–4 garlic cloves, crushed,
    or 2 teaspoons garlic paste
    (page 59)
½ teaspoon ground turmeric

TO SERVE
¼ bunch of fresh coriander
    (cilantro), leaves and stems
    roughly chopped
Roti (page 57), Rice (page 28)
    and a few other curries

Peel and dice the potatoes into small cubes (around 1–2 cm/½–¾ inch) and place in a bowl of cold water to stop them oxidising.

Heat the oil in a large frying pan (you'll need one that has a lid) over medium heat, then add the onion, chilli, curry leaves and whole spices and cook until the onion starts to turn golden brown, about 4–5 minutes. Add the garlic and turmeric and cook for 30 seconds. Drain the potato and add to the pan with a little pinch of salt and give everything a good mix. Cover with a lid and cook, stirring every couple of minutes (or more if it's sticking), until the potato is tender enough to break up with a spoon, about 25–30 minutes.

Taste and adjust with salt. Garnish with the coriander and serve with roti, rice and other curries, or spoon some onto a roti, roll it up and place it in a lunch box.

EGG CURRY (page 66)

Potato Curry (page 67)

(Machli Tarkari) Fish Curry

SERVES 4–6 × ACTIVE TIME 20 MINUTES × TOTAL TIME 35 MINUTES

This recipe is part of the set of OG, unadulterated recipes that I want to pass on to my kids. When I was little, my mum's favourite fish to use in this curry was from Fiji. We'd smuggle it into Australia frozen and wrapped in newspaper. None of us have done a side-by-side comparison with locally caught fish, but my family is convinced the Fiji fish is better. In Australia, my favourite is Spanish mackerel, which is widely available.

Mum washes all her seafood in vinegar or lemon. It makes the fish firmer. Interestingly, it's the opposite of what you usually want in Western cooking, where you want it to be soft, flaky and melt in your mouth. For a curry, you need it to be set, so it doesn't break apart.

100 ml (3½ fl oz) white vinegar
6 Spanish mackerel cutlets
   (600–700 g/1 lb 5 oz
   –1 lb 9 oz)
2 tablespoons plain
   (all-purpose) flour
⅓ cup (80 ml) light olive oil
1 small brown onion,
   thinly sliced
1 sprig fresh curry leaves
1 teaspoon The Mixture
   (page 60) or ¼ teaspoon
   each of cumin seeds and
   black mustard seeds, and
   ⅛ teaspoon fenugreek seeds
10 garlic cloves, crushed,
   or 1½ tablespoons
   garlic paste (page 59)
10 g (¼ oz) fresh ginger, finely
   grated, or 1 teaspoon
   ginger paste (page 59)
1 tomato, diced
1 teaspoon ground turmeric
½ teaspoon chilli powder
2 tablespoons Fiji masala
   powder
25 g (1 oz) fresh tamarind
   soaked in 100 ml (3½ fl oz)
   warm water (see tip,
   page 61) or 1 tablespoon
   store-bought tamarind paste
300 ml (10½ fl oz) hot water
100 ml (3½ fl oz) coconut
   cream

TO SERVE
1 small bunch of fresh
   coriander (cilantro), leaves
   and stems roughly chopped
Roti (page 57) and Rice
   (page 28)

Combine the vinegar and 2 cups (500 ml) water in a bowl. Wash the fish in the vinegar mixture, drain and pat dry with paper towel. Sprinkle the fish with the flour and a pinch of salt.

Heat ¼ cup (60 ml) oil in a frying pan over medium heat, then add the fish and fry until GBD (see page 13), about 2 minutes each side. (No need to cook the fish through, just aiming to get colour.) Set aside on a plate.

Wipe the pan clean with paper towel, then add the remaining oil along with the onion, curry leaves and whole spices. Cook over medium–high heat. When the onion starts to turn golden brown, add the garlic, ginger and tomato and cook until the tomato breaks down, 3–5 minutes. Add the powdered spices and a pinch of salt and cook out for 1–2 minutes.

Now, mix in the tamarind paste, then cook for another 2 minutes. Add the hot water and bring to a gentle simmer. Cook for 5 minutes, then add the seared fish and let it cook for 5 minutes. Pour in the coconut cream and simmer for 2 minutes.

Season with salt to taste and garnish with the coriander. Serve with roti and rice.

(Bhindi Tarkari)
Okra Curry

SERVES 4-6 × ACTIVE/TOTAL TIME 30 MINUTES

Bindi, okra, lady's fingers, whatever you want to call it, is my mum's favourite curry (along with jackfruit and the duck curry my dad made). Back in the day, it wasn't as easily available as it is now, but it was prized in our house. Every time we saw it in an Asian grocers, we'd buy it. It does seem to be one of those things people either love or hate — probably because of the slimy texture — but when you cook it in a pan with a little oil like this, you don't get that.

2 tablespoons light olive oil
½ brown onion, thinly sliced
1–2 fresh chillies, halved
    lengthways
1 sprig fresh curry leaves
1 teaspoon The Mixture
    (page 60) or ¼ teaspoon
    each of cumin seeds and
    black mustard seeds, and
    ⅛ teaspoon fenugreek seeds
4 garlic cloves, crushed, or
    1 tablespoon garlic
    paste (page 59)
1 kg (2 lb 4 oz) okra, cut into
    1 cm (½ inch) pieces

TO SERVE
Roti (page 57), Rice (page 28)
    and a few other curries

Heat the oil in a frying pan over medium heat, then add the onion, chilli, curry leaves and whole spices and cook until the onion starts to turn golden brown. Add the garlic and cook for another 1–2 minutes. Add the okra and a pinch of salt and cook, stirring occasionally, until the okra has softened, about 15–20 minutes.

Serve with roti and rice and, of course, a few other curries.

Green Bean Curry (Bean Tarkari)

This is an easy way to use a mass of beans. My family had beans in the backyard, so we always had a lot to use. Growing up I thought it was normal. I thought every Fijian-Indian grew their own beans in the backyard. We would even play a game when driving into a new suburb: if we saw a bean tree, a curry leaf tree and a banana tree we'd go, 'Yeah, that's an Indian family's house.'

2–3 tablespoons light olive oil
½ brown onion, sliced as
    thin as you can
2–3 bird's eye chillies,
    halved lengthways
15–20 fresh curry leaves
1 teaspoon The Mixture
    (page 60) or ¼ teaspoon
    each of cumin seeds and
    black mustard seeds, and
    ⅛ teaspoon fenugreek seeds
3–4 garlic cloves, crushed,
    or 2 teaspoons garlic paste
    (page 59)
½ teaspoon ground turmeric
1 kg (2 lb 4 oz) green beans,
    quartered lengthways
    and cut into 2–3 cm
    (¾ –1¼ inch) lengths

TO SERVE
Roti (page 57), Rice (page 28)
    and a few other curries

Heat the oil in a frying pan over medium heat, then add the onion, chilli, curry leaves and whole spices and cook until the onion starts to turn golden brown. Add the garlic and turmeric and cook for 30 seconds. Now, add the beans, season with a pinch of salt and cook until the beans have softened, about 20–25 minutes.

Taste and adjust with salt. Serve with roti, rice and a few other curries.

(Jheenga Tarkari) Prawn Curry

SERVES 4-6 × ACTIVE/TOTAL TIME 30 MINUTES

My brother's favourite curry — potentially his favourite food of all time — is prawn curry. When I was a kid, my mum made this a lot, but now she's somehow become allergic to shellfish. But if my brother comes over, Mum will put on gloves, smash an antihistamine and make prawn curry for the whole family. If that's not love, I don't know what is.

There are two ways to make this. There's this recipe, which is for a dry curry, or you can add coconut milk to make a creamier version. For the creamy, coconutty one, just double the powdered spices and pour in 200 ml (7 fl oz) each of canned coconut cream and water when you add the prawns (see tip). I like to serve the creamy version with rice and the dry version with roti.

I usually keep the prawn shells and heads on; they have so much flavour — particularly the head, which has this savoury-sweet prawn stock flavour. You can do on or off, whatever you like, but if you're doing the coconut cream version, I'd recommend shells on. They add heaps to the broth.

1 kg (2 lb 4 oz) local king
    prawns (see tip)
¼ cup (60 ml) light olive oil
1 brown onion, roughly diced
2 bird's eye chillies
1 teaspoon The Mixture
    (page 60) or ¼ teaspoon
    each of cumin seeds and
    black mustard seeds, and
    ⅛ teaspoon fenugreek seeds
5–6 garlic cloves, crushed,
    or 3 teaspoons garlic paste
    (page 59)
5 g (⅛ oz) fresh ginger, finely
    grated, or ½ teaspoon
    ginger paste (page 59)
6–8 fresh curry leaves
1 teaspoon ground cumin
1 teaspoon ground turmeric
1 teaspoon Fiji masala or
    garam masala
½ teaspoon chilli powder
1 tomato, roughly diced

TO SERVE
1 small bunch of fresh
    coriander (cilantro), leaves
    and stems roughly chopped
Roti (page 57) and Rice
    (page 28)

Clean the prawns by removing the poop shoot. If you want to keep the shell on, do this by finding a gap in the shell near the head, inserting a skewer and pulling out the shoot. Otherwise, peel the prawns, leaving the tails intact.

Heat the oil in a large frying pan over medium heat, then add the onion, fresh chilli and whole spices and cook until the onion starts to turn golden brown, about 4–5 minutes. Add the garlic, ginger, curry leaves and powdered spices. Cook for about 2–3 minutes, then add the tomato and cook for 1–2 minutes until it breaks down.

Now, add the prawns and mix so they are evenly coated with the spice mixture. Taste and adjust with salt (about 2–3 pinches or 1½ teaspoons) and cook until the prawns are just cooked through, about 5–7 minutes (longer if they're shell on; cook until the shells have turned orange).

Garnish with coriander and serve with roti and rice.

TIPS If you're making the creamy version, keep the prawn heads and shells on to impart more flavour into the curry.

To pick the best prawns, look at the integrity of the shell and antennas. If the antennas are still on and still long, then the prawns haven't been handled and tossed around as much. Also, always go for local prawns.

Cabbage Curry (Gobi Tarkari)

SERVES 4–6 × ACTIVE/TOTAL TIME 30 MINUTES

In my head, there is a gang of curries, all these different characters, but they all stick together. Chicken curry is the leader. There's potato curry, egg curry and cabbage curry in there too. There's a hierarchy, but I don't know what it is. Look, this is dumb, but I've just run out of ways to explain how I enjoy curry. I do think cabbage is having a bit of a moment. Everyone is charring it and caramelising it in miso, but stir-fried with spices is great. It's a veg that takes on a lot of flavour, so it's amazing in a curry.

¼ cup (60 ml) light olive oil
½ brown onion, thinly sliced
1 bird's eye chilli, halved
    lengthways
8–10 fresh curry leaves
1 teaspoon The Mixture
    (page 60) or ¼ teaspoon
    each of cumin seeds and
    black mustard seeds, and
    ⅛ teaspoon fenugreek seeds
3–4 garlic cloves, crushed,
    or 1½ teaspoons garlic
    paste (page 59)
2 teaspoons ground turmeric
1 teaspoon ground cumin
½ cabbage, thinly sliced

TO SERVE
1 small bunch of fresh
    coriander (cilantro), leaves
    and stems roughly chopped
Roti (page 57), Rice (page 28)
    and a few other curries

Heat the oil in a frying pan over medium heat, then add the onion, chilli, curry leaves and whole spices and cook until the onion is golden brown, about 2–5 minutes. Add the garlic and cook for another minute.

Now, add the turmeric, cumin and a generous pinch of salt and mix well. Add the cabbage and mix in too. Cook, stirring periodically (around every 5 or so minutes), until the cabbage becomes tender (you still want a tiny bit of bite), about 15–20 minutes.

Season to taste, garnish with the coriander and serve with roti, rice and a few other curries.

Dhal Bhat, the Fancy
Version (page 81)

The OG Dhal Bhat
(page 80)

Dhal Bhat, the Pinnacle

My mum and my grandma made dhal literally every day, but it was never the same. They didn't have a recipe. If they didn't have eggplant (aubergine), they wouldn't use them. Sometimes they added garlic, other times they played around with different kinds of lentils. It was always different, and it was always amazing. Dhal is the pinnacle of Indian comfort food. Whenever I go home to visit, Mum will make dhal, chicken curry, roti and rice. She knows they're still my favourites.

But even though it was such a fond recipe, I didn't make it until I was in the *MasterChef* apartment practising for challenges. I didn't know what was going to happen on the show, but I wanted this up my sleeve so I could make something that meant a lot to me during a challenge. So, I called my mum. I had no regard for time at that point in my life. It was probably midnight in Melbourne, she was in Sydney and I hadn't seen her in months.

Mum: What is it like over there?

Me: Mum, I just want to know how to make dhal.

I was moving around the kitchen, phone to ear, Mum telling me what to do. She gave a vague description, but I'd eaten it a thousand times, so when she said something as confusing as, 'Add this, it'll taste better,' I knew what she meant.

Me: Yeah Ma, I think it's finished.

Mum: How's it taste?

Me: Good.

Mum: Okay, that's good. Goodnight.

That's how it was. Mum taught me the traditional version, but I wanted to make a creative one on the show — something new, but still nostalgic. So, I tried making a crisp from dehydrated rice, making a thicker dhal you could use as a dip and adding pickled onions and chutney for more texture, acidity and pops of spice. I practised in the apartment, but I only nailed it on TV. It was super weird to do it in front of the whole world, but that's the kind of cooking I wanted to share with people. The humble recipes I grew up with.

First up is The OG — a culmination of all I learned from Mum and Grandma. If it's like their dhal, it'll be perfect. The second recipe is my *MasterChef* recipe.

The OG Dhal Bhat

½ cup (100 g) red lentils
½ cup (100 g) yellow lentils
1 teaspoon ground turmeric
1 teaspoon salt
1 carrot, peeled and
    finely chopped
1 small eggplant (aubergine),
    peeled and finely chopped
1 tomato, finely chopped
2 teaspoons lemon juice
    (from about ¼ lemon)

TEMPER
2 tablespoons ghee
1 small brown onion,
    finely chopped
1 garlic clove, finely chopped
1 bird's eye chilli, halved
    lengthways (use ½ or
    ¼ if you want less spice)
1 teaspoon The Mixture
    (page 60) or ¼ teaspoon
    each of cumin seeds and
    black mustard seeds, and
    ⅛ teaspoon fenugreek seeds

TO SERVE
Roti (page 57), The OG
    Chicken Curry (page 84)
    and Chilli Chutney
    (page 218)

Wash the lentils and place in a saucepan with 5 cups (1.25 litres) water. Bring to a simmer and cook for 10 minutes, stirring after 5 minutes. Skim and discard any white foam that comes to the surface. Stir in the turmeric and salt until combined, then add the carrot, eggplant and tomato. Simmer until the lentils are soft (you should be able to easily crush one between your fingers), about 10–15 minutes. Using a potato masher, give the dhal a rough mash to thicken.

To make the temper, heat the ghee in a frying pan over medium–high heat, then add the onion, garlic, chilli and whole spices and cook until the onion is golden brown.

Add the temper to the dhal and mix in, then season with the lemon juice and more salt to taste.

Serve with roti, chicken curry and chilli chutney.

Dhal Bhat, the Fancy Version

SERVES 4 × ACTIVE TIME 35 MINUTES × TOTAL TIME 1 HOUR 35 MINUTES

½ cup (100 g) red lentils
½ cup (100 g) yellow lentils
½ teaspoon ground turmeric
1 tomato, finely chopped
1 carrot, peeled and
    finely chopped
30 g (1 oz) unsalted butter
1 small brown onion,
    finely chopped
1 garlic clove, thinly sliced
½ bird's eye chilli,
    roughly diced
½ teaspoon cumin seeds
¼ teaspoon fennel seeds
1 tablespoon lemon juice
    (from about ½ lemon)

BASMATI RICE CRISP
½ cup (100 g) basmati rice

QUICK PICKLED ONION
½ red onion, thinly sliced
¼ cup (60 ml) white vinegar

CORIANDER CHUTNEY
1 bunch of fresh coriander
    (cilantro), leaves and stems
1 garlic clove
1 long green chilli
1 bird's eye chilli
1 tablespoon lemon juice
    (from about ½ lemon)
1 tablespoon extra virgin
    olive oil
1 teaspoon white vinegar

To make the basmati rice crisp, wash the rice until the water runs clear. Transfer to a small saucepan with 1 cup (250 ml) water. Bring to a simmer, then cover with a lid and cook until the rice is slightly overcooked, about 20 minutes. Drain.

Preheat the oven to 140°C (285°F). Line a baking tray with baking paper.

Blitz the rice in a blender until you get a smooth, thick paste, adding a little water if it's too thick to blend. Spread the blitzed rice as thin as possible over the prepared tray. Sprinkle salt over the rice, then bake until crisp, about 1 hour. (If it browns, you've gone too far; you don't want any colour.) Set aside.

Meanwhile, make the quick pickled onion. Place the red onion, vinegar and a generous pinch of salt in a bowl. Use your hands to massage everything for 1–2 minutes, then set aside for 20 minutes to pickle.

While the onion is pickling, wash the lentils, then place in a saucepan with 3 cups (750 ml) water. Bring to a simmer and cook for 10 minutes, stirring after 5 minutes. Skim and discard any white foam that comes to the surface. Stir in the turmeric and a pinch of salt until combined, then add the tomato and carrot. Simmer until the lentils are soft (you should be able to easily crush one between your fingers), about 10–15 minutes. Using a potato masher, give the dhal a rough mash to thicken.

Heat the butter in a frying pan over medium heat, then add the onion, garlic, bird's eye chilli, cumin and fennel seeds and cook for 2 minutes. Mix this butter mixture into the lentil mixture. Adjust the seasoning with the lemon juice and salt to taste. Using a stick blender, roughly blitz the dhal to slightly thicken it (you want the consistency of a chunky hummus).

To make the coriander chutney, roughly chop the coriander, garlic and green and bird's eye chillies, then transfer to a blender along with the remaining ingredients. Blend until smooth, then season with salt (you're looking for something with a bit of punch; it should be spicy and a little sour).

Place the dhal in a serving bowl, then top with the chutney and a few slices of pickled onion. Break the rice crisp into iPhone-sized shards and serve on the side.

I Am Curry

My mum's chicken curry means a lot to me. It's usually the first thing I cook for people — it's like my introduction; how I tell people who I am.

It was my favourite dish growing up, but I wasn't always comfortable sharing it with others. When I had friends come over, I'd always ask Mum to make lasagne, chicken wings or anything but curry. One day, we had a study day at my house and all these other kids came over and when they walked in, Mum was making chicken curry for our family dinner. I was so embarrassed, but my friends could smell it and wanted to know what it was. My mum asked if they wanted to try it. From then on, Mum made curry every study night. It was the first Indian food my friends had and the first they fell in love with. It helped me feel more comfortable with who I am.

On *MasterChef*, you're asked to create a signature dish, something that represents you and something you're going to be known for. The obvious choice for me was chicken curry. I still remember the judges eating it for the first time, saying it was epic, talking about how much they loved it and saying I had potential. All those years ago I was embarrassed by it and now I've cooked it in front of the entire world! It was a turning point in my life. The fact that it was this dish, my mum's chicken curry, that opened the door to this new world is crazy and poetic.

'One thing I like about my two boys: no matter what they cook or what they make, they always come home for chicken curry, roti, dhal and rice. Justin will make the chicken curry in whatever way, but it's always Mum's chicken curry that's his favourite.'

- Justin's Mum

(Murgi Tarkari)
The OG Chicken Curry

**SERVES 4–6 × ACTIVE TIME 50 MINUTES × TOTAL TIME 50 MINUTES
+ 30 MINUTES MARINATING**

Don't tell my grandma this, but I think my mum is the alpha cook in the family. She learned from both her mum (nani) and from my dad's mum (parti), who she lived with for 24 years. Through osmosis — how you really learn to make Indian food — she gained the skills and recipes from two of the most incredible cooks I know. This is her original chicken curry, my death row meal.

It isn't a creamy curry. It's dry, fresh and light. In South India, which is roughly where my family originates, that's the style. Instead of coconut milk, tomato or dairy, the moisture comes from the chicken and its bones. It creates a chicken stock-like gravy and gives you a really intense, savoury flavour.

Oh, soy sauce? I know. Everyone is like, what the heck? But it makes sense. Soy sauce is just saltiness, umami and a bit of colour. It snuck into Mum's cooking when she came to Australia. I don't know if other Fijian-Indian families are doing it. I just know my family is.

1 whole chicken (1.2–1.5 kg/
    2 lb 12 oz–3 lb 5 oz,
    see tip)
1 tablespoon lemon juice
    (from about ½ lemon)
1 tablespoon soy sauce
¼ cup (60 ml) light olive oil
1 teaspoon The Mixture
    (page 60) or ¼ teaspoon
    each of cumin seeds and
    black mustard seeds, and
    ⅛ teaspoon fenugreek seeds
1 brown onion, roughly diced
    or sliced
1 sprig fresh curry leaves
3–4 garlic cloves, crushed,
    or 2 teaspoons garlic
    paste (page 59)
10 g (¼ oz) fresh ginger, finely
    grated, or 1 teaspoon
    ginger paste (page 59)
1½ teaspoons ground
    coriander
1 teaspoon ground cumin
1 teaspoon ground turmeric
1 teaspoon chilli powder

TO SERVE
½ bunch of fresh coriander
    (cilantro), leaves and stems
    roughly chopped
Roti (page 57) and Rice
    (page 28)

Using a heavy cleaver or sharp knife and some muscle, break down the chicken into roughly 3–4 cm (1¼–1½ inch) pieces, keeping the meat on the bone. (You can also ask the butcher to do this.) Place the chicken pieces in a bowl with the lemon juice and soy sauce and mix. Let it sit for 30 minutes (this will keep the chicken firm during the cooking).

Heat the oil in a large saucepan over medium–high heat, then add the whole spices and toast until fragrant, about 1 minute. Add the onion and cook until it starts to turn golden brown. Add the curry leaves, garlic, ginger and powdered spices and cook for 1–2 minutes. Add the chicken and the soy marinade and mix in. Season with a little pinch of salt, cover with a lid and cook, stirring periodically (every 5–10 minutes), for 20–30 minutes.

Taste and adjust with salt. Garnish with the fresh coriander and serve with roti and rice.

TIPS For a little more depth of flavour and spice, finish off the curry with 1–2 teaspoons Chilli Chutney (page 218) or serve it on the side and everyone can add their own.

If you don't want to break down a whole chicken or you want a boneless curry (I won't judge you), just sub it out for 800 g–1 kg (1 lb 12 oz–2 lb 4 oz) skinless, boneless chicken thighs.

As pictured on page 86

That was the food I grew up with; Parti and Mum's rogue and resourceful Fijian version of Indian food.

The OG
Chicken Curry (page 84)

The 'Chicken Curry' that
Got me a Masterchef Apron (page 88)

The 'Chicken Curry' That Got Me a MasterChef Apron

SERVES 4 × ACTIVE/TOTAL TIME 1 HOUR 30 MINUTES + 1–4 HOURS MARINATING

You know that scene in *The Bear* where the chef breaks down a Chicago deep-dish pizza? What do you think they would do to a chicken curry? This is kind of that idea: elevating the plating, but keeping it authentic to what it is. There are three elements: a pork crackling-like chicken skin crisp, a juicy piece of chicken breast — breast gets a lot of hate, but if you cook it perfectly, it's the best cut of the chicken (controversial, I know) — and a cauliflower puree that makes everything really lush. The idea is, unlike a regular curry, every bite is a different experience.

Honestly, this does take a bit of time. So, if you have some on your hands and you're trying to earn major brownie points with someone, this is the dish to cook.

1 whole chicken (1.2–1.5 kg/
    2 lb 12 oz–3 lb 5 oz)
½ teaspoon garam masala
½ teaspoon smoked paprika
2 garlic cloves, crushed, or
    1 teaspoon garlic
    paste (page 59)
2 tablespoons light olive oil
Pinch of ground turmeric
15 g (½ oz) unsalted butter

CURRY SAUCE
1 tablespoon grapeseed oil
1 large brown onion,
    roughly sliced
4 garlic cloves, roughly sliced
10 g (¼ oz) fresh ginger,
    roughly sliced
1 long red chilli, roughly sliced
1 bird's eye chilli,
    roughly sliced
1 teaspoon cumin seeds
1 teaspoon coriander seeds
½ teaspoon fennel seeds
1 tomato, roughly chopped
2 cups (500 ml) chicken stock
1 teaspoon light soy sauce
1 small bunch of fresh
    coriander (cilantro), leaves
    and stems roughly chopped
1 tablespoon lemon juice
    (from about ½ lemon)
5 g (⅛ oz) unsalted butter

Pat dry the chicken with paper towel. To separate the chicken skin, slice along the backbone of the chicken, then using your fingers, push under the skin to separate it from the flesh and work your way around the chicken. Once removed, set aside the skin.

Remove the breasts from the chicken by cutting down along the centre breastbone, then along the carcass. Remove the thighs and wings (reserve these for another use) and set aside the carcass with the skin. Place the breasts in a bowl with the garam masala, paprika, garlic, half the olive oil, a few cracks of black pepper and a pinch of salt and marinate, covered, in the fridge for 1–4 hours.

Preheat the oven to 200°C (390°F). Line a baking tray with baking paper.

Lay the reserved skin flat on a board, with the inside of the skin facing up, and scrape away any excess fat. Transfer the skin to the prepared tray, laying it flat. Sprinkle with the turmeric and a pinch of salt, then lay another sheet of baking paper on top. Place another baking tray on top to weigh it down. Set aside.

Using a cleaver, break down the reserved chicken carcass into manageable chunks. Lightly coat in the remaining olive oil and transfer to a roasting tin. Roast both the carcass pieces and chicken skin for 30–40 minutes until both are GBD (see page 13) and the skin is crisp.

To make the curry sauce, heat the grapeseed oil in a frying pan over medium–high heat, then add the onion and cook until golden brown, about 5 minutes. Add the garlic, ginger, chillies and whole spices and cook for 1–2 minutes until softened. Add the tomato, carcass pieces and the fond (the browned and caramelised bits stuck to the bottom of the roasting tin). Cook for a further 1–2 minutes. Cover with the stock, soy sauce and 300 ml (10½ fl oz) water and bring to a simmer. Cook until the mixture reduces by two-thirds, about 30–40 minutes, periodically skimming to remove any impurities or fat that pools on top.

CAULIFLOWER PUREE
½ head cauliflower, roughly
    chopped
2 cups (500 ml) milk
15 g (½ oz) unsalted butter

QUICK APPLE PICKLE
1 green apple, diced
¼ teaspoon chilli powder
1 teaspoon white vinegar
¼ teaspoon salt

TO SERVE
Chilli Chutney (page 218)
Flaky sea salt, to season

Add the fresh coriander and 1 teaspoon lemon juice to the pan. Let that simmer over medium–high heat for 5 minutes, then strain the mixture, discarding the solids. Pour the mixture back into the pan. While stirring constantly, add the butter and simmer until it's the texture of thick cream. Taste and adjust with salt and more of the lemon juice if it needs it (you just want to balance the richness and saltiness). Reduce heat to low and keep warm until you're ready to plate (or warm just before serving).

Meanwhile, take the chicken breasts out of the fridge and allow them to come to room temperature. Now, make the cauliflower puree. Heat a saucepan over medium heat. Add the cauliflower and milk and bring to a simmer. Cook until the cauliflower is soft enough to crush with the back of a spoon, about 20 minutes.

While the cauliflower simmers away, make the quick apple pickle. Mix all the pickle ingredients in a bowl and let it sit for 20 minutes.

Drain the cauliflower, reserving the liquid. Transfer the cauliflower to a blender and blitz until smooth, adding some reserved liquid until you have a thick, yoghurt-like consistency. Add the butter, season with salt and a few cracks of black pepper and blitz again.

Heat a cast iron frying pan over medium heat, then sear the marinated chicken breasts until lightly golden brown, about 2 minutes each side. Add the butter, then transfer the pan to the oven and roast for 6–8 minutes until cooked through. (If you have a probe, you want to pull it out at 68°C/155°F.) Allow them to rest for 5 minutes.

Cut the chicken breasts in half lengthways, drain the pickled apple and break the crispy chicken skin into shards. On one side of each serving plate, place 2 tablespoons of the curry sauce, then drizzle 1 teaspoon of oil from the chutney over the sauce. Place a chicken breast piece, cut side up, on top of the sauce. Top with a shard of crispy skin and a pinch of flaky sea salt. On the other side of each plate, place a generous tablespoon of cauliflower puree and 3 × ½ teaspoon mounds of apple pickle around it.

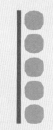

Roast Chicken Curry

SERVES 4–6 × ACTIVE TIME 15 MINUTES × TOTAL TIME 45 MINUTES + 2 HOURS–OVERNIGHT MARINATING

El Jannah and Frangos (two Sydney charcoal chicken institutions) inspired this recipe, which probably sounds weird because this is a curry. It's got that familiar spatchcocked roast chicken technique and appearance, but then it's got the flavours of a curry. I guess this is a more modern way of plating and eating a curry but honestly, for me, it's the minimal effort maximum return way of making chicken curry. Instead of getting a huge pot and stirring a curry for half an hour, you can just bang the chicken in the oven or on the barbecue.

If your mates are coming over, it's so easy to put this on. Get some cos lettuce and dress it with mayo and lime, and that's it, meal done. Or, if you want to make it sexy and fancy it up, serve with some condiments and make **Masala Roast Potatoes (page 153)**, **Chunky Cucumber Raita 'Salad' (page 47)** and **Coconut Buns (page 53)**. Epic meal.

It's best to start this the day before but, I'll be honest, I've done a 30-minute marinade and it was still great.

1 whole chicken (1.2–1.5 kg/
2 lb 12 oz–3 lb 5 oz)

MARINADE
1 tablespoon lemon juice
(from about ½ lemon)
1 tablespoon soy sauce
¼ cup (60 ml) light olive oil
15–20 fresh curry leaves
¼ brown onion,
roughly chopped
5–6 garlic cloves, roughly
chopped, or 3 teaspoons
garlic paste (page 59)
15 g (½ oz) fresh ginger, finely
grated, or 1½ teaspoons
ginger paste (page 59)
1½ teaspoons ground
coriander
1 teaspoon ground cumin
1 teaspoon salt
2 teaspoons ground turmeric
1 teaspoon chilli powder

TO SERVE
Fresh coriander (cilantro)
leaves, roughly chopped
Rice (page 28) or your
favourite sides

Start by spatchcocking the chicken (page 118).

Blitz all the marinade ingredients in a blender until you have a smooth paste. Pat dry the chicken with paper towel, then smother with the marinade and really massage it in. Allow it to marinate, covered and in the fridge, overnight (or for a minimum of 2 hours or less if you can't be bothered).

Take the chicken out of the fridge and allow it to come back to room temperature.

Meanwhile, preheat the oven to 220°C (430°F).

Place the chicken, breast side up, and the marinade in a baking dish or cast iron frying pan, then in the oven and roast until the chicken is cooked through and slightly charred, about 25–30 minutes. Allow it to rest for 10–15 minutes, then carve up the chicken (for tips, see page 119).

Garnish with any resting juices from the dish and fresh coriander. Enjoy with rice or your favourite sides.

TWO

LOVE, ENTERTAINMENT, HUNGER, PRESSURE: EVERYTHING THAT MADE ME COOK

Most people in Australia get their food education from TV, I reckon, from shows like *Huey's Cooking Adventures*, *Ready Steady Cook* and all the Gordon Ramsay series. For me, the big ones were Jamie Oliver's *The Naked Chef* (he was the first young, cool chef on TV) and, genuinely, *MasterChef*. My grandparents, Parti and Tata, and I watched every episode of at least the first five seasons. And this was before catch-up TV; we were committed.

My grandparents and I were very close. Watching cooking shows was one of the ways we bonded. We'd have live commentary running; we'd chat about what the cooks were making and how they'd made it, and we had a game where we'd try to guess what they were going to make. Usually, it was something we'd never heard of, and our minds would be blown seeing it all come together. Even things like risotto or cuts of meat like a filet mignon — we'd never seen anything like that. My grandparents were learning about Australian culture and I was learning about cooking. Sometimes my grandma would scribble down a recipe or I would see something I liked and I'd say to Parti, 'Let's try and make that!' Then, the next time we were at the store and we saw an ingredient from TV we'd buy it, go home and make whatever Jamie Oliver cooked. It was our way to assimilate.

Cooking shows taught me about the possibilities of what you could do with food, but what got me into the kitchen and cooking on my own was wanting to make food for my family. Mum had a tradition of cooking our favourite meals on our birthdays. It always made us feel special and I wanted to return that, I wanted her to feel special too. So, it started with me volunteering to make breakfast in bed for Mother's Day. Then, I'd be asking my parents what they wanted to eat on their birthdays. For Mum, it was usually a mushroom risotto, for Dad it was steak. It escalated from there.

I didn't start cooking Indian until I moved out of home to live in Perth when I was 25. That was the first time in my life I wasn't eating Mum's or Parti's cooking. We were literally on opposite sides of the country, and I missed home and their food. Learning to cook the food I grew up with was my way of curing my homesickness. I would call Mum and Dad most days, and when I spoke to Mum I would be asking her how she makes everything. At the same time, I started thinking about Parti. She was getting old and I was thinking about all the food she made, all the memories I had of her and how they would one day just fade away. I started feeling like I had a responsibility to learn her recipes and to continue her story, our family traditions and her food. I wanted to be able to pass it on to my kids one day.

In Perth, I was cooking a lot, not just my mum and parti's recipes, but everything I was seeing on TV and YouTube. I was doing big barbecue cook-ups, Mexican experiments and *Chef's Table*-inspired several-course fine dining meals. But I never thought about cooking being my career. It was a hobby and something I was good at — even something I was known for — but I never thought I was that good. I'd see what people on *MasterChef* did and I'd think it was impossible. It was like watching magic. I thought I'd never be able to do that. Sure, people had told me they liked my food, but they were family and friends, people who already backed me. I just discredited what they said.

Going on *MasterChef* changed everything. One thing I hadn't taken into consideration when I was sitting at home with my grandparents watching TV with our minds blown, was how much the contestants learn. For seven months I was away from my family, my job, everything. My whole universe was cooking. I had access to every ingredient from every cuisine, I was surrounded by people constantly thinking about food and I had these amazing mentors — not only the three judges, but also whoever else came in to guest-judge (some of the best chefs in Australia and the world). The amount of knowledge that gets condensed into those seven months is crazy. It's one of the best culinary intensives you can get.

But what I gained on *MasterChef* wasn't just experience and a concentrated pill of culinary knowledge, it was validation. I thought I was just scraping through until the challenge to get into the top ten. I remember the judges trying my Vanilla Coke-inspired dessert (a Vanilla Coke ice-cream with Coke jelly, and a salt and vinegar chocolate disc) and saying it was unbelievable, the best dish of the day. From then on, I was in a flow state. I started enjoying it more. I had mojo (that sounds weird, but it's genuinely how I felt) and my internal monologue was just me saying, you're going to crush this. Even during the pressure tests, when there were like 100 steps to do in a limited time, I just thought, I love pressure tests, I'm going to dominate. I may not have believed that the entire time, but I had great people around me — the judges, other contestants, my family and friends — all instilling this belief in me, so I said it to myself until I believed it too. All I had needed was for someone from that world, the world I'd grown up watching on TV, to tell me I was good enough. That gave me full permission to go for it.

The recipes in this chapter are the first recipes I started cooking. To you, they may seem like a random mishmash of cultures, cuisines and techniques, but for me, they're all the same. They're Australia, my backyard and the culture I grew up with. They're some of the first recipes to give me confidence to cook for other people and maybe they can help you do the same.

Driver's Licence Lamb Cutlets

SERVES 4 × ACTIVE TIME 10 MINUTES
TOTAL TIME 15 MINUTES + 2 HOURS–OVERNIGHT MARINATING

I remember the first time I cooked this. My grandparents lived with my family most of my life, but when I was 17, they moved out. We'd spend most weekends visiting them and I'd always tell them, 'When I get my licence, I'll come and visit you.' They'd say, 'Yeah sure, you'll forget.' After getting my licence, my first trip was to their house to cook them lunch. I went to the local IGA and got some lamb cutlets. We always used to have lamb in curries, but we never had premium cuts. We were just familiar with them from all the ads on TV. I marinated them in yoghurt and spices I found rummaging around in my grandparents' cupboards — yoghurt-based marination wasn't the norm, it's more of a North Indian thing and my family history is in the South. I pan-fried them and smoked the whole house out. We sat outside, ate couscous salad and lamb cutlets. They didn't say anything, but I know they loved it.

The reason I remember this recipe is not because it's groundbreaking. It's because it's been a few years now since my last visit to see them. Tata passed in 2013 and Parti passed in 2022, but I'll never forget what I cooked them when I got my driver's licence.

600–800 g (1 lb 5 oz–
    1 lb 12 oz) lamb cutlets
    (about 12 cutlets)
3–4 garlic cloves, crushed,
    or 2 teaspoons garlic paste
    (page 59)
1 teaspoon smoked paprika
1 teaspoon ground cumin
½ teaspoon Fiji masala powder
    or garam masala
1 teaspoon chilli flakes
2 tablespoons Greek-style
    yoghurt

TO SERVE
Extra virgin olive oil
Lemon wedges
Flaky sea salt, to season

Pat dry the lamb with paper towel. Place everything in a bowl with a good pinch of salt and mix well. Cover, then allow it to marinate in the fridge for 2 hours or overnight (overnight will give you more tender and flavoursome meat).

Half an hour before you want to cook, remove the lamb from the fridge and discard any excess marinade (keep the marinade on the lamb).

Either fire up a barbecue to medium–high or heat a cast iron frying pan over medium-high heat (open up all the windows, trust me). Grill the lamb, in batches if needed, until nicely charred, about 3–4 minutes each side (if you have a probe, remove the lamb from the heat at 58°C/136°F). Allow them to rest for 5 minutes.

Plate up and garnish with a drizzle of olive oil, a squeeze of lemon and a pinch of flaky sea salt.

Oysters Kilpatrick

MAKES 12 × ACTIVE TIME 10 MINUTES × TOTAL TIME 20 MINUTES

Oysters Kilpatrick was the first way I tried oysters. Dad would have ordered it when we went out for dinner ages ago. Mum never had any — she doesn't eat oysters — but after a while, she started cooking it for my dad at home. He would go to the fish markets, buy oysters and ask if she could make it. That's what always happened in our house. Whenever someone wanted to eat something, they would buy the ingredients and bring them over. I remember my uncle coming over, he'd bring a crab or something and my grandma would say, 'Okay, I'll cook it for you.' That's just the way love was exchanged in the house.

2 tablespoons tomato ketchup
2 tablespoons Worcestershire
    sauce
1–2 dashes Tabasco, to taste
1 tablespoon balsamic vinegar
12 oysters
3 streaky bacon rashers,
    finely chopped

TO SERVE
Fresh flat-leaf parsley leaves,
    finely chopped (optional)
Lemon wedges

Preheat the oven grill to its highest temperature.

Meanwhile, mix all the sauces and vinegar in a bowl until combined. On a baking tray, place a sheet of foil that's larger than the tray and slightly scrunch it up, so you can nestle the oysters in the scrunched folds to keep them in place. (You can also use rock salt.) Gently place all the oysters in the foil.

Top each oyster with a teaspoon of the sauce mixture and about a teaspoon of chopped bacon. Place under the grill and cook until the bacon is crisp and GBD (see page 13), about 5–10 minutes.

Sprinkle with parsley, if using, and serve with lemon wedges on the side.

Sizzler Cheese Toast

MAKES 4 PIECES × ACTIVE/TOTAL TIME 10 MINUTES

Sizzler was one of the greatest culinary institutions in Australia until it sadly came to an end in 2020. We used to go as kids whenever it was our birthday. What I liked about it: there were no rules. You get given a plate and the world is your oyster. It changes the way you think about life; just for a brief moment you can have whatever you want, right now. Go to the salad bar, load up on bread, get dessert with ice-cream and jelly. As a kid, that's crazy. There are very few places and times in your life where you can do that. Imagine going to a shopping mall and someone gives you a trolley and says you can go fill it up as much as you want. I feel like there is a life lesson in this somewhere, but I don't know what it is. There's no moral, it's just get whatever you want and stuff yourself.

It didn't surprise me that it closed. I hadn't been in 20 years, but I was still devastated. I felt a bit responsible. I should have gone more so my kids could have had the same experience I had.

Anyway, the Sizzler toast is iconic. It's thick-cut white bread (nothing special), untoasted on one side and salty, garlicky and crispy on the other side. The hack is to have it upside down, so all the flavours hit your tongue rather than the roof of your mouth. I reckon everyone should be doing this with garlic bread too, way better experience. I was feeling nostalgic one day, so I made it at home. It was amazing. #Sizzler4eva!

100 g (3½ oz) unsalted butter, softened
40 g (1½ oz) parmesan, finely grated
1 teaspoon garlic powder
4 thick-cut slices (1.5–2 cm/⅝–¾ inch) white bread (buy an unsliced loaf and slice it yourself)

Place everything, except the bread, in a bowl. Add a few cracks of black pepper and a pinch of salt and mix until smooth and everything is evenly combined. Spread a thick layer of the cheesy butter over each piece of bread.

In a cast iron frying pan over low heat, place the bread, cheesy butter side down, and toast until crisp and GBD (see page 13), about 2–3 minutes. Then remove from the pan. You'll have one side perfectly crispy and the other side perfectly steamed. Take a bite and shed a tear as you realise one of the greatest things in this world hasn't been lost.

The Bagel

MAKES 6 × ACTIVE TIME 30 MINUTES
TOTAL TIME 1 HOUR 20 MINUTES + 1 HOUR 10 MINUTES PROOFING

Remember when everyone was into sourdough during lockdown? My mate Harry got weirdly into bagels. Probably because his wife is American and there were no bagels around, so he made his own. Anyway, he nailed it and ... well, basically I stole it.

The classic toppings:
- Cream cheese, smoked salmon, heaps of capers and thinly sliced red onion.
- Bacon, egg and American cheese.
- Smashed avo with pepper, lemon and feta.

300 ml (10½ fl oz) warm water
2½ teaspoons (10 g) active
   dry yeast
1 heaped tablespoon (20 g)
   caster (superfine) sugar
500 g (1 lb 2 oz) plain
   (all-purpose) flour,
   plus extra for dusting
1 teaspoon (6 g) salt
Light olive oil, for greasing

MILK WASH
½ cup (125 ml) milk
2 tablespoons of a mix of
   poppy seeds, sesame seeds
   and black sesame seeds
   (or 2 tablespoons bagel
   seasoning or omit and
   leave it plain)

Mix the warm water, yeast and sugar in a bowl. Let it sit for 10 minutes.

Combine the flour and salt in a large bowl, then add the yeasty water (all at once is fine) and mix until the mixture is shaggy. Spread extra flour over a clean work surface and knead the dough until smooth and bounces back (poke it lightly to test), about 10–15 minutes. (You can also do this in a stand mixer with a dough hook.)

Grease a bowl with some oil, spreading it around to make sure the dough doesn't stick. Place the dough in the prepared bowl, cover and let it rest in a warm spot for 45 minutes–1 hour (it should double in size).

Punch the dough to let the air out. Divide into six equal pieces and shape each into a tight ball. Cover all the balls with a clean tea (dish) towel and allow them to rest for 5–10 minutes.

Meanwhile, preheat the oven to 220°C (430°F) and line a baking tray with baking paper. Bring a large saucepan of water to a simmer.

Grab each dough ball and poke your thumb through the centre to create a hole, then work your thumb around the hole to make sure the dough is even all around (they should look like bagels). Carefully lower each one into the pan (do this in batches if you need) and simmer for 30–45 seconds each side. Remove the bagels from the water, place them on the prepared tray, brush with the milk, then sprinkle with the seed mix, if using. Bake until golden brown, about 20–25 minutes.

Allow to cool slightly and enjoy the endless possibilities of the bagel.

The Omelette

SERVES 1 × ACTIVE/TOTAL TIME 10 MINUTES

I love *The Hundred-Foot Journey*. There's a scene in the film where the main guy, a chef from India, goes to France. He ends up making an omelette for a fine dining chef. It's this intense scene with lots of eye contact between him and Helen Mirren. He nails it and she offers him a job at her restaurant the next day. That's like a folk tale in the chef world; how you judge a chef is how well they can make a perfectly silky omelette. That was the first thing I'd ever seen with a young, cool Indian chef, so of course, I saw myself in the film. The Indian chef was me. So, the next day it was time to learn how to nail an omelette. There were so many failed attempts, rips and tears, but I got really into it. I went through a phase where I was eating them almost all the time – breakfast, dinner, whatever – just because I was trying to practise. What it teaches you is heat control. You have to take the pan on and off the heat; you can't just leave it there. To nail it you need to cook intuitively.

3 eggs
15 g (½ oz) unsalted butter
   (the best quality you
   can find), plus extra
   to serve (optional)

TO SERVE
Flaky sea salt, to season
Fresh chives, finely chopped
   (optional)

Crack the eggs into a bowl and beat them with a whisk or fork until they're combined. Get a plate out for serving, this will go quickly.

Heat the butter in a non-stick frying pan over medium heat. Once the butter is melted and starting to froth, pour in the egg. Using a rubber spatula, constantly move the egg in a gentle, whisk-like motion. (Make sure to scrape the side of the pan, moving the egg into the centre.) If any holes or gaps in the egg showing the bottom of the pan appear, tilt the pan so the egg runs into that section. When the egg is slightly cooked (looking like liquidy cottage cheese on top), stop stirring and let the egg set for 20–30 seconds. If you want to add any extra fillings (see tip), do it now by putting them all on one side of the egg, the side furthest from you. At this point, the centre will still be runny, but the edges will be starting to set. Turn off the heat and season the top of the egg with salt and pepper.

With the pan handle facing you, tilt it up (so the handle goes towards your chin) and get the spatula under the egg on your side, then fold about a third of the egg inwards. Get the spatula under the folded layer and fold that over the last bit of unfolded egg. Take the pan over to your plate, tilt the egg side of the pan down towards the plate and gently flip the omelette onto the plate so it's seam side down. Using paper towel or a clean tea (dish) towel, shape it into a perfect cylinder. If you want, rub the outside with extra butter – that's what I do. Hit it with flaky sea salt, sprinkle with chives, if using, then that's it, you've made an omelette.

TIP For fillings, think about the omelette like it's two pieces of bread. Anything can go in there. One time I did a cheeseburger omelette with leftover burger ingredients. I fried off minced (ground) beef before I made the omelette, then put the mince, American cheese and pickles on the egg as it was about to set.

Cooking Steak at 13: From Non-Stick to Cast Iron

When I was growing up, whenever it was someone's birthday we'd go out. The kids would pick Sizzler or Pizza Hut, Mum would pick Chili's (a Tex-Mex restaurant that's not around anymore) and my dad would pick a steak house — his favourite was Lone Star.

He told us this story about it. He went out on a business trip to a country town with a workmate and they ended up at a Lone Star. My dad had never had a steak, but he's adventurous so ordered exactly what his mate got: a medium-rare steak with hot English mustard and mashed potatoes. He loved it, so whenever we went to Lone Star he would order a medium-rare steak and he'd tell us about the steak he had in the country town. We'd never eaten anything like that either, but we'd try it with Dad. He was like the pioneer of the family. My mum was always horrified. 'How do you eat that?!' Mum and Dad grew up in Fiji where the meat quality was quite poor, so they mostly cooked the crap out of everything. She couldn't handle meat that was slightly pink or had blood in it.

When I was a teen, my family had some difficult times and our lifestyle dramatically changed. We went from going to restaurants and ordering whatever we wanted to almost never going out. We lost a lot, but we never lost the connection in our family unit. I think subconsciously that informed my habits.

At that time I was watching a lot of cooking shows, like Jamie Oliver's *The Naked Chef* and *Ready Steady Cook*. I'm seeing these guys cooking steak and they made it look so easy. I was about 13, but I thought I could replicate it. The next time we went to the shops, I saw steak was cheap — cheaper than the restaurant — and I connected the dots. I said to my parents, 'Let's get steak. I'll cook tonight. We can have mushroom sauce and mashed potatoes.' I was 13, but it wasn't foreign for me to be in the kitchen. My brother and I would help prep, do dishes, all kinds of stuff. So, from Mum's perspective, I had it covered. Dad was pumped. Without looking at the thickness or the marbling (I didn't know anything about the quality of a steak), I got a T-bone, because that's what Dad liked. I took it home and whacked it in a non-stick pan. Something I would never do again.

My parents have always been encouraging, but I know they like something if they request it again, and every Father's Day or birthday after that my dad would ask for steak. I think it was a way for me to love my dad. I grew up seeing my mum and grandma do that, and cooking became my way of doing that for my friends and family. Steak was the gateway dish.

I like how steak shows my progression as a cook. When I first made it, I was getting a thin T-bone from a supermarket, sticking it in a non-stick pan and seasoning it with iodised table salt. Now I'm getting Rangers Valley Wagyu porterhouse steaks with marbling scores of MB7. I'm using high quality, flaky sea salt, I have a meat probe and a cast iron pan and I can cook a steak by feel.

Dad and I never go out for steaks anymore. We know we can cook a better one at home for a fraction of the price. He got out of hospital recently and when I asked him what he wanted to eat, he said steak, so I went out and got the best steak I could.

How to Cook the Perfect Steak

This is an edited version of a conversation I've had with a lot of friends, trying to educate them on how to cook a steak.

HOW TO BUY A GOOD STEAK

Stuff getting individual steaks for each person. Get one big steak for everyone. It's better and easier. Focus your energy on just cooking that one thing.

Different cuts will work for different needs (more on that below). The main things to look for are thickness and marbling.

Thickness

You need a thick steak to get a good crust, which is where all the flavour is. If the steak is too thin, you will overcook the centre by the time it gets a really good crust. You want something at least two fingers thick — that's my rule, but if you want to be exact, around 4–6 cm (1½ –2½ inches).

Marbling

Fat equals flavour, that's why you need marbling. Fat will also help keep the steak juicy if you go a bit over or under — the leaner the cut, the more you have to cook it to perfection. Generally, the higher the marbling the better, but you can go too high. A steak with a marbling score of MB9 will be the best steak you ever have in your life for one bite but, like good quality butter, you can't eat a whole block — it is amazing on toast though. For a big steak, I would go MB4 to MB7.

Grain or grass fed

Grain-fed beef is higher in fat, but grass-fed has a more complex flavour. It's also better for you, so I usually go grass-fed. A grass-fed, grain-finished steak is also a great option.

Dry aged or not

Dry ageing is basically hanging cuts of meat up in a fridge with air circulating around it. As it loses moisture, the flavour intensifies. The other big benefit, because of the lack of moisture, is the crust you get. A good dry-aged steak is unbelievable, but they're very expensive. My qualm with them is the waste. When you dry age meat, the outside of it gets a pellicle (a hard piece of meat that you can't eat), which needs to be discarded. Give it a go once, but for the everyday steak, I'm not going to buy it. I'd rather spend the extra money on better quality meat and dry it out for 24–48 hours in my fridge on a wire rack.

The best cut and the best and worst value cuts

The best cut in my opinion is the rib eye cap, aka spinalis dorsi. My two favourite producers in Australia are Rangers Valley and O'Connor.

I think the best value is a grass-fed rump cap, aka picanha. There is a big difference between a rump and rump cap. The rump is the tough bottom end. The rump cap is that top end, which doesn't move as much, so it's way more tender. The flavour is insane for the price, and it has an epic amount of fat on it.

Filet mignon is the worst value for money. It's very tender (like incredibly tender, it doesn't do any work), but there's no flavour. It's only good if you pour sauce all over it, but if I buy beef I want to taste beef.

Where to buy

The thickness you need cancels out most supermarket retailers. For the best steak, go to a good butcher. I would encourage you to develop a good relationship with your local. They know all their products, they can give you tips and tricks and they can often point to something cheaper and better. If you can't find what I'm telling you to buy, they'll suggest the next best thing.

HOW TO PREP A STEAK

If you have time, do a dry brine — that will get the best results.

Dry brine

Put the steak on a wire rack and heavily salt both sides from a height so you get an even distribution. Use the best quality cooking salt you have.

Put it in the fridge and leave it for two hours minimum. There's no such thing as too long — the best result is overnight. In that time the salt will draw out the moisture, then the salt will dissolve into the moisture and the steak will reabsorb it, seasoning the inside of the steak.

Take it out of the fridge 20—30 minutes before you're gonna cook to get it to room temperature. Get a paper towel or clean tea (dish) towel and pat the steak completely dry. You don't need to rub it, just pat it. The pat dry is essential — moisture is the enemy of a good crust.

No time quick method

If you don't have time for a dry brine, you can salt just before you're going to cook. Get the steak to room temperature, pat it dry and season it with a good pinch of best quality cooking salt (from a height, so you get an even distribution) on each side, then cook straight away.

How to cook it

If you're starting out, use a frying pan instead of a barbecue. It's easier to control and more consistent. Coals have incredible flavour, but barbecuing adds another layer of complexity to the cooking. I say the best way to cook a steak is medium-rare and these instructions are for that.

What pan to use

The best way to cook steak is with a cast iron frying pan. It stays hotter for longer and the hotter the surface, the better crust you get and the better flavour you get. Stainless steel is the next best thing. Non-stick is horrible — throw it out.

Heating and oiling the pan

Preheat the pan to the highest heat you have for 5 minutes. You want the pan as hot as you can get it — you should see it smoke. Not getting the pan hot enough is the most common issue for home cooks. I think many are afraid of having it too hot, and most domestic kitchens usually don't have burners that even get it that hot.

If you have a bit of fat on the side of the steak, start by holding the steak with the fat side down on the pan. You're going to render that fat and use that as the oil. If you don't have extra fat to use, put a little grapeseed or another high smoke point oil in (the fat in the pan helps you get an even heat and crust). Don't use butter — it burns at the temperature you want.

Basting

If you get a good quality steak, you don't need to baste it. It will have enough fat inside. I don't usually baste my steaks. It helps introduce another flavour and if the steak is super thick it helps get an even cook, but I don't think it gets you a better steak.

Flipping and taking the steak off the pan

I flip my steaks every 15—20 seconds, which is the Heston method. He says it cooks the steak more evenly and you get an edge-to-edge pink. I agree. I also find it gives you a better crust. The idea is the side of the pan with no steak is conducting a lot of heat, so when you flip, you flip to the empty side of the pan, always putting the steak onto the hottest part of the pan.

If the pan isn't hot enough, don't be afraid to take the steak off and rest it on a plate while the pan heats up again. I don't know why, but people seem afraid to do that. It's fine.

Timing by heat probe

There are too many factors to give an exact cooking time: the thickness of the steak, the burners you use, your pan, etc. The most consistent way is to use a probe. Invest in a good one. It takes out all the guesswork around timing. Get the probe in the centre and pull the steak off when it's at 48°C (118°F).

Timing by feel

I cook by feel, literally prodding the steak in the pan with my finger. What you're looking for is a steak that has a bit of give, but a bit of bounce. If you press your middle finger lightly to your thumb and feel the muscle at the base of your thumb, that's the texture of medium rare. If you go to the ring finger, that's well done. It's different for every steak, but a two-finger steak is going to be generally about 4 minutes a side.

HOW TO REST AND CARVE

When you remove the steak from the pan, it will continue cooking, with the centre of the steak rising around 5°C (41°F). Those extra 5°C are important because what makes a steak juicy is the fat melting, and the melting point of beef fat is 50–55°C (120–130°F).

Resting

If you cut into the steak as soon as you take it off the heat, the fat and meat juices will ooze out. Resting it keeps the fat in and gives you a more even cook. If you have a meat probe, rest the steak until it gets to 55°C (130°F). If you don't have a probe, rest it for the same amount of time you cooked it, unless it's a big steak and you did a long cook, then rest for half the time.

Carving

If you've done everything right up until this point, the steak will have that edge-to-edge pinkness and a great crust. To carve, look at the beef — the muscle fibres run one way. You want to cut against the muscle fibres, which will make it more tender. Cutting with the grain is going to be a bit chewy. For visuals and ease of sharing, I like to slice my steak in slices about 1–1.5 cm (½–⅝ inch) thick.

Seasoning and using the resting juices

After you've carved, sprinkle some flaky sea salt over the steak. It gives you texture and some nice pops of salt as you eat. If you're worried the steak has cooled down too much, heat the resting juices in the pan then pour those on. If you've already used the resting juices, you can heat some butter or sauce and pour that over instead.

WHAT TO SERVE IT WITH

Condiments wise, go with whatever you like: red wine sauce, mushroom sauce, a pepper sauce, anything. Dad loves hot English mustard. I've used chilli chutney too. I don't pour it over the steak. I have a little jug or bowl of it on the side, so everyone can use the sauce at their discretion. I like a good sauce but honestly, I'm a steak purist. Everyone has worked hard to make this steak so good (also steak isn't cheap), so I like to taste the beef.

Sauces

Mushroom sauce was my introduction to making sauces. It was part of the original Lone Star-inspired meal that I made for my dad (page 104) – steak, mashed potato and mushroom sauce – and it's still my go-to.

I think stainless steel is the best pan for sauces. You can see the fond (the sticky, caramelised bits on the bottom of the pan), then either deglaze or scrape it off to use. If you're making a steak sauce for the first time, make it ahead of time. While your steak rests, use the steak pan to heat up the sauce.

As for what sauce goes with what, you can do whatever, but this is what I do:

- **Mushroom (below):** Classic with steak, chicken schnitty, grilled fish and grilled chicken.
- **Diane (opposite):** Great with steak and chips.
- **Red Wine (opposite):** Best for steak, chicken and pork.
- **Chimichurri (page 112):** Steak, seafood and chicken, but this particularly goes with anything.
- **Peri Peri (page 112):** Chicken sandwich, prawns, hot chips and, of course, Portuguese-style charcoal chicken (page 168).
- **Curry Leaf Butter (page 230):** Delicious with chicken, steak and seafood.
- **Chilli Chutney Butter (page 230):** Very versatile, so great with everything.

Mushroom Sauce

SERVES 2–4 × ACTIVE/TOTAL TIME 20 MINUTES

I honestly think any mushrooms would work, but a combination will give you a more complex flavour. I usually do button and Swiss brown, because they're affordable.

1 teaspoon light olive oil
15 g (½ oz) unsalted butter
300 g (10½ oz) mushrooms, sliced
2 garlic cloves, crushed
1 teaspoon Dijon mustard
200 ml (7 fl oz) chicken stock
1 teaspoon Worcestershire sauce
  (light soy sauce also works)
1 cup (250 ml) thickened (whipping) cream
2–3 sprigs fresh thyme
1 teaspoon white wine vinegar

Place a stainless steel frying pan over high heat, then add the oil and butter. When the butter is melted, add the mushroom and shake the pan to distribute evenly, get as many as you can flat on the pan. Just leave them for 2–3 minutes to get that Maillard reaction (if you stir them, they will sweat and release moisture).

Once they've got a good sear, give them a stir (hopefully getting all the opposite sides hitting the pan) and, while stirring, cook for another 2 minutes. Add the garlic and cook for another 30 seconds, then add the mustard, stir and cook for another 30 seconds. Add the stock and Worcestershire and bring to a simmer. Reduce by half, then add the cream and thyme. Bring to a simmer and cook, periodically stirring, until reduced by one-third and coats the back of a spoon.

Add the vinegar, salt and pepper to taste. Remove the thyme sprigs to serve.

Diane Sauce

SERVES 2–4 × ACTIVE/TOTAL TIME 20 MINUTES

You know the fancy date where you go to a French restaurant and get steak frites? Cook a steak and make this sauce at home and you can have the same experience while sitting on the couch watching *The Proposal* with someone you love (see tip).

15 g (½ oz) unsalted butter
1 French shallot, finely chopped
1 garlic clove, finely chopped
1½ teaspoons Dijon mustard
1 teaspoon tomato paste (concentrated puree)
50 ml (1½ fl oz) brandy or cognac
1 cup (250 ml) beef stock
2 teaspoons Worcestershire sauce
100 ml (3½ fl oz) thickened (whipping) cream
3–4 drops sherry vinegar (red wine vinegar works too)
¼ bunch of fresh chives, finely chopped

Place a stainless steel frying pan over medium–low heat, then add the butter, shallot and a little pinch of salt and cook for 1–2 minutes. Add the garlic and cook for another minute, then the mustard and tomato paste. Cook for 1–2 minutes.

Now, for the fun part. Add the brandy or cognac and get ready to flambé. You can either tilt the pan and expose the sauce to the flame or hit it with a kitchen blowtorch or lighter. (If you use a lighter, get ready to do the quick withdraw technique.) When the flame goes down, add the stock and Worcestershire and reduce by half. Pour in the cream. Reduce until thick enough to coat the back of a spoon (reduced by about half again). Add the vinegar. Season with salt and pepper. Take off the heat and add the chives.

Red Wine Sauce

SERVES 2–4 × ACTIVE/TOTAL TIME 20 MINUTES

The better the red wine, the better the sauce, but any red wine works. Use whatever you have. If you want a recommendation, I use cab sav or pinot noir.

1 French shallot, finely chopped
40 g (1½ oz) cold unsalted butter
(the best quality you can find)
1 garlic clove, roughly chopped
300 ml (10½ fl oz) red wine
1 cup (250 ml) beef stock
1 sprig fresh thyme

Place a stainless steel frying pan over medium–high heat, then add the shallot and half the butter and cook until the shallot is translucent, about 2 minutes. Add the garlic and cook for another minute, then pour in the red wine and reduce by two-thirds, about 3–4 minutes. Add the stock and thyme and reduce everything again by two-thirds, about 10 minutes.

Once everything has reduced, strain the sauce into a small saucepan. Reduce the heat to medium and, while mixing constantly, slowly add in the rest of the butter (the mixing helps it emulsify). Taste the sauce and season with salt, if needed.

TIP For a sexy little steak and frites, air-fry or deep-fry some frozen shoestring fries according to packet instructions. Pour a generous amount of Diane Sauce onto a plate and top with a perfectly cooked steak (page 106), then place the fries atop the steak.

Chimichurri

SERVES 4–6 × ACTIVE/TOTAL TIME 10 MINUTES

I don't know how authentic this is, but it tastes good. I think the thing that makes a good chimichurri is good quality extra virgin olive oil, getting the right balance of acidity and taking the time to finely chop everything. You can pulse it in a food processor, but it will emulsify a little. I like the texture and look of a hand-chopped chimichurri. Any leftovers will keep in the fridge for 24–48 hours.

3 garlic cloves
1 French shallot
1 bird's eye chilli
1 small bunch of fresh flat-leaf parsley,
    leaves and stems
1 small bunch of fresh coriander (cilantro),
    leaves and stems
100 ml (3½ fl oz) extra virgin olive oil
1 tablespoon red wine vinegar
1 tablespoon lemon juice (from about ½ lemon)

Take your time to finely chop all the fresh ingredients. Mix the fresh ingredients with the remaining ingredients in a bowl and season with flaky sea salt and pepper to taste. (Alternatively, roughly chop all the fresh ingredients, place all the ingredients in a food processor and pulse until finely chopped and smoothish.)

Peri Peri

SERVES 4–6 × ACTIVE/TOTAL TIME 5 MINUTES

The garlic powder, rather than fresh garlic, makes this sauce. It gives it a thick, creamy texture and a more mellow, savoury garlic flavour.

3 teaspoons garlic powder
4 bird's eye chillies
4 red cayenne chillies
1 tablespoon lemon juice (from about ½ lemon),
    plus extra to taste
Pinch of caster (superfine) sugar
100 ml (3½ fl oz) extra virgin olive oil
½ teaspoon salt

Place all the ingredients in a blender and pulse until everything has emulsified into a creamy, delicious sauce. Adjust seasoning with salt and extra lemon juice, if needed.

The Smash Patty Cheeseburger

MAKES 4 × ACTIVE/TOTAL TIME 30 MINUTES

I was a McDonald's Cheeseburger Happy Meal kid. Now, as an adult, I'm still a classic cheeseburger guy. Sometimes you want a greasy meal (you kind of want to feel a little dirty), and a cheesy hits the spot. I feel like in recent times there has been somewhat of a smash burger renaissance and for good reason, it's the superior burger. I wanted to make a recipe that has a bit of a McDonald's vibe, but takes on the smash burger technique in a way that can be easily replicated at home. You don't need any smashing tools, you just need body weight, a baking tray and a well-seasoned cast iron frying pan. Once you make a good burger, you will get a lot of confidence.

500 g (1 lb 2 oz) minced
    (ground) beef (80:20 meat
    to fat, see tip)
Neutral high smoke point oil,
    for frying
4 slices American cheese

BURGER SAUCE
2 tablespoons Whole Egg Mayo
    (page 226 or store-bought)
1 tablespoon Heinz Tomato
    Ketchup
2 teaspoons American mustard
1 teaspoon apple cider vinegar

TO SERVE
4 brioche burger buns or
    potato buns, halved
16 dill pickle slices
½ brown onion, finely chopped

To make the burger sauce, combine all the sauce ingredients and a small pinch of freshly cracked black pepper in a small bowl. Mix well.

Divide the beef into four even balls (125 g/4½ oz each if you want to be exact). Using scissors, cut eight pieces of baking paper into 8 × 15 cm (3¼ × 6 inch) rectangles. Place each ball between two pieces of baking paper and, one by one, get a baking tray or heavy saucepan and press down using your body weight to flatten the ball. Aim for roughly 0.5 cm (¼ inch) thick. Remove the tray or pan but leave the baking paper on. Now you have four smashed burger patties.

Heat a small drizzle of oil in a frying pan over high heat. Peel off the top layer of paper from one patty (or more patties depending on the size of your pan) and place, meat side down, in the pan. Remove the second layer of baking paper and season the patty with a pinch of salt and pepper. Cook until you have a deep golden brown crust, about 3–4 minutes. Flip (it should have cooked 80–90 per cent of the way through). Place a slice of cheese on the patty (it should be sitting on the crust side). Wait for the cheese to start melting, about 30 seconds, then remove from the pan and set aside on a board or plate. Repeat with the remaining patties.

In the same pan, toast both sides of the buns, cut side down, until golden brown, around 10–30 seconds.

To assemble, place each patty on top of a bun base. Add the pickle slices, top each with 1 tablespoon burger sauce and sprinkle with the onion. Add the bun top halves and get into it.

TIP Get the best quality mince you can from your local butcher. If you are getting it ground there, ask for 50:50 chuck to short rib. If you're going to the supermarket, make sure you don't get the expensive lean stuff. You want the regular fatty mince (it's usually 80:20 meat to fat, which is what you need here).

Choose Your Own Adventure Slow Braise Osso Buco or Lamb Shanks

SERVES 4 × ACTIVE TIME 30 MINUTES × TOTAL TIME 4 HOURS 30 MINUTES

Bone marrow gives both of these dishes their richness and depth of flavour. The gremolata (a zesty herb sauce) brings balance to the richness. Traditionally, osso buco (the inspiration for this recipe) would have celery. I've made this dish with celery and without celery, and it just doesn't add much. It melts into nothing. Also, I don't want to have any connection to celery. Pointless ingredient.

This is one of those easy bulk recipes. You can cook it ahead of time, leave it in the oven and go do your own thing during the day.

4 pieces osso buco or
    4 lamb shanks
1 tablespoon plain
    (all-purpose) flour
1–2 tablespoons light olive oil
1 brown onion, roughly diced
1 carrot, roughly diced
1 tablespoon tomato paste
    (concentrated puree)
300 ml (10½ fl oz) pinot noir
    or whatever red you have
2 cups (500 ml) chicken stock
6 garlic cloves
2–3 sprigs fresh thyme
2–3 sprigs fresh rosemary
2–3 sprigs fresh sage

GREMOLATA
Handful of fresh flat-leaf
    parsley leaves
    (about 20 g/¾ oz)
1 garlic clove
2 anchovies, finely chopped
¼ cup (60 ml) extra virgin
    olive oil
1 lemon, zested and juiced
    to get 2 tablespoons

TO SERVE
Buttery mashed potatoes

Preheat the oven to 170°C (325°F).

Pat dry the osso buco or shanks with paper towel. Sprinkle with the flour, a pinch of salt and a few cracks of black pepper. Heat a drizzle of light olive oil in a Dutch oven or ovenproof saucepan over high heat. In batches, sear the meat on both sides until deeply GBD (see page 13), about 2–4 minutes each side. Remove the meat and set aside. Add the onion, carrot and tomato paste to the pan and cook for 2–3 minutes. Pour in the wine and bring to a simmer. Add the stock, seared meat plus any resting juices, garlic and herb sprigs. Take off the heat, put the lid on the pan and place in the oven for 3–4 hours or until the meat can be cut with a spoon.

While the meat is in the oven, put all the gremolata ingredients, using 30 ml (1 fl oz) of the lemon juice, in a food processor and pulse until everything is finely chopped. (Alternatively, if you want the therapy or to practise your knife skills, finely dice everything the best you can.) Season with salt and more of the lemon juice to taste — it should be fresh and a little sour and salty.

Take the pan out of the oven. If the broth isn't a good sauce consistency, remove the meat from the pan and set aside while you bring the broth to a simmer on the stove over medium heat until reduced (thick enough to coat the back of a spoon). Taste and adjust with salt. Return the meat to the pan.

Serve the osso buco or shanks with mashed potatoes, topped with the gremolata.

Roast Crispy Pork Belly

SERVES 4–6 × ACTIVE TIME 20 MINUTES
TOTAL TIME 2 HOURS 20 MINUTES + 1–2 DAYS DRYING

Crispy skin pork belly is just one of those mystical and wonderful foods. I fell in love with it through siu mei (Chinese barbecue) after my dad was introduced to it by a Singaporean friend. He used to go to a shop in Eastwood (a suburb in north west Sydney) to get it and when he brought it home, it was always perfectly crispy. It inspired me to go on a quest to make the perfect crispy pork belly.

For a long time, I thought it was impossible. I did so many attempts and tried so many recipes — I tried foil wraps, covering it in salt, the vinegar brushing method and cooking it on the skin and flipping it over. Some methods worked better than others, but none of them had a consistent, crispy skin. It was never as good as what we got from the siu mei shop. Years later, I found out the secret when I was working in a restaurant famous for its porchetta. They had this unreal crispy skin on the pork and the secret was hanging it up to dry in the walk-in cooler room for two days before cooking it.

This recipe is the best way to do it at home. Serve with your favourite sides or save it for sandwiches, tacos or banh mi. And if you have any left over, make Sisig (page 179)!

700 g–1 kg (1 lb 9 oz–
  2 lb 4 oz) pork belly
  (see tip)
½ teaspoon freshly cracked
  black pepper
1½ teaspoons flaky sea salt

OPTIONAL FLAVOURINGS
½ teaspoon chilli flakes
1 teaspoon fennel seeds
½ teaspoon coriander seeds

Dry the pork belly thoroughly using paper towel. Using a clean Stanley knife set to a length that will pierce the fat but not the flesh, score the skin with a 0.5 cm (¼ inch) gap between each cut. The safest way to do this is to start in the middle and cut away from yourself. If you don't have a Stanley knife, you can use a sharp chef's knife or a skewer to poke as many holes as you can in the top (making sure you only pierce the skin and not the flesh).

To dry out the skin, leave uncovered in the fridge for 1–2 days (usually the top shelf is the best ventilated and you want airflow to dry it out as much as possible). You should be able to see the skin dry out over this time.

If you want to flavour the pork, place all the optional flavourings into a spice grinder or use a mortar and pestle and grind coarsely.

Preheat the oven to 170°C (340°F).

If you're using optional flavourings, rub those on the meat side of the pork. Otherwise add a few cracks of black pepper, then sprinkle with salt. Arrange the pork belly, skin side up, on a baking tray so the skin is flat and even. If it isn't, use scrunched-up foil or bits of raw onion underneath the meat to level it out. Heavily salt the pork skin, then place it in the oven to roast for 50 minutes–1 hour (the slow roast will render the fat and give you juicy, tender meat). A 1 kg (2 lb 4 oz) cut will need a little longer than the 700 g (1 lb 9 oz).

Remove the pork from the oven. While the pork rests, increase the oven to 250°C (480°F). Once the oven reaches temperature, place the pork back in the oven and roast until you have that crispy crackle on the skin, about 20–30 minutes (keep an eye on it).

Remove the pork from the oven and let it rest for 20–30 minutes. Place the pork, skin side down, on a chopping board and slice.

TIP When you're buying pork belly, look for the most even bit of the pork belly — this will help get a consistent crispy skin. Also, I like to get the meatiest bit I can. There's plenty of fat in the cut, I don't think it needs any more.

How to Cook the Perfect Chicken

Every culture seems to have their own barbecued or roast chicken recipe. Once you master the technique of roasting chicken you can try any of them, the possibilities are endless.

HOW TO BUY A GOOD CHICKEN

What chicken you buy makes a big difference in both flavour and texture. When you buy a cheaper chicken, you get a caged bird and breed that grows very fast. It's usually slaughtered young, which means it has a subtle flavour. General rule of thumb: the older something gets, the more flavour it develops. Look for a free-range chicken with unbroken skin (you want that skin to crisp up and you also need it to protect the meat from drying out). If you want to be really bougie, get a free-range, corn-fed chicken. It has beautiful yellow skin and a deeper chickeny flavour.

Also, look for a decent, medium-sized bird. I like to go between 1.2–1.5 kg (2 lb 12 oz–3 lb 5 oz). Once it's over that size, it's hard to handle.

HOW TO PREP A CHICKEN

Spatchcocking

When you roast a whole chicken, the bottom part can be soggy and the skin never renders properly and doesn't get crisp. Whereas, spatchcocking a chicken exposes all the skin to the heat, giving you a much crispier result. It also halves the cooking time.

The first step is to remove the wishbone, which is at the top of the breasts, where the neck would have been. If you follow the line of the breast around the cavity of the chicken, you should be able to feel it. Get a knife in the cavity of the chicken, press the blade against

the wishbone and scrape along the bone (you should hear the knife when it hits bone) to separate the meat from the bone. Repeat on the other side, then you should be able to pull the bone out with your fingers. It's hard to describe — you can always watch a YouTube video, that's what I tell my friends to do.

With kitchen scissors, remove the backbone by cutting along either side of it. While you have the scissors, remove the wing tips (they don't have much flavour and in the heat you'll be cooking them with, they'll just burn). I keep the backbone and wing bones in a ziplock bag in my freezer and when I have enough, I make stock (they're high in gelatine, making them excellent for stock).

Now lay the chicken skin side up and give it a push so it lays flat (you want the surface to be as even as possible).

Marinade

Choose your own adventure, literally — you can put anything in a marinade. For ideas, check out the 'Charcoal' Chicken and Toum (page 166), Frangos Style Chicken (page 168), Jerk Chicken (page 170) and Buttermilk Roast Chicken (page 121). Simply massage the marinade into the chicken and put it in the fridge, covered, overnight. Like a dry brine, you can do a shorter time (2 hours minimum), but overnight will give you the best result.

Dry brine

If you want to roast chicken for future meal prep — for salads, sandwiches or whatever — I would do a dry brine instead of a marinade.

Salt the underside (not the skin side) of the chicken, making sure it's evenly spread. I do a good pinch (around ½ teaspoon). Flip it over, place it on a wire rack, pat the skin with a paper towel to dry it, then salt the skin side. Leave it overnight in the fridge, uncovered and skin side up (this will help dry the skin). The salt will pull all the moisture out from the flesh and skin (if you look after an hour, it will look really wet). After some time, the moisture and salt will slowly reabsorb back into the chicken, seasoning the inside and drying out the skin, helping you get a more flavoursome chicken and crispier skin.

When you're ready to cook, give the top (skin side) just a little drizzle of oil and rub it over the chicken.

COOKING

Preheat the oven to 240°C (475°F). Hit the chicken with a sprinkle of nice flaky sea salt. Transfer it to a baking dish and into the oven. The back part of the oven tends to be the hottest, so go legs first (drumsticks pointing to the back of the oven). They have more fat, so they can take more heat. If you've got a bird that's between 1.2–1.5 kg (2 lb 12 oz–3 lb 5 oz), roast for about 25–30 minutes.

Check by feel
Look at the skin. If it's golden brown, that's the first good sign it's done. There may be some charred bits or some skin a bit bubbled up, that's normal. You can also feel the chicken breast to see if it's done. You're looking for the feel of the ring finger in the steak test: place the tip of your thumb to the tip of your ring finger to tense the muscle, then feel the muscle at the base of your thumb (you want your chicken to have a similar firmness).

If you're starting out, it's better to pull your chicken out early and undercooked, because you can always cook it more.

Check by probe
Probe at the thickest part of the breast and thigh. When the breast is about 60°C (140°F) and the thigh is 65°C (150°F), it's time to pull out the chicken. Keep in mind, it will continue to cook another 5–8°C (41–46°F).

RESTING AND BREAKDOWN

Resting
Let it rest for 10–15 minutes, which sounds like a long time, but it's been in a hot oven and there's a lot of residual heat, so the chicken will continue to cook. After 10 minutes it will still be warm and juicy. If you have a probe, you want the breast to be 68°C (154°F) and the thigh to be 74°C (165°F) when it's finished resting.

Breakdown
You can break it down however you like but honestly, I never understand people who carve a chicken like a Christmas turkey. Why do people do that? Anyway, I usually break it down into eight pieces, which serves four people — two big pieces each (one breast and one piece of dark meat). To do that, cut between the breasts, separating the two halves of the chicken. Cut the thigh off the breast as close to the joint as you can, trying to keep the skin on the breast piece. Remove the drumstick from the thigh, again trying to get as close as you can to the joint. Cut halfway across the breast. I like to go on an angle, so you get the wing on one end and most of the meat on the other end.

Pinkness
When you break down the chicken, you shouldn't see any pink meat, but if you cut into the joint of the thigh and drumstick and the bone is a bit pink, that's totally fine. If this is unpleasant to your guests, just get a frying pan over high heat and kiss the pink piece of the chicken bone on the hot pan. You can also do the same with a kitchen blowtorch or by putting it back in the oven.

SERVING
If there are any resting juices in the baking dish, pour those over the chicken pieces. If the juices need to be warmed up, just chuck them in a pan.

Buttermilk Roast Chicken

**SERVES 4–6 × ACTIVE TIME 20 MINUTES × TOTAL TIME 1 HOUR
+ 4 HOURS–OVERNIGHT MARINATING AND 15 MINUTES RESTING**

This recipe happened by accident. I wanted to make buttermilk fried chicken. I had the chicken brining in buttermilk and I went to season it with salt and pepper. I was grinding pepper with one of those cheap pepper grinders, but nothing was coming out. Instead of grinding, I was loosening the lid. I gave it a shake and everything fell into the buttermilk. So annoying. I just put everything in the fridge to think about later. When I came back to it, I just couldn't be bothered to pick out the peppercorns, dredge and deep fry it. I thought, I'm just going to roast it, see what happens.

My updated version is to also add garlic to the buttermilk, then blitz the roasted buttermilk sauce with the chicken juices. You get this thickened cream consistency, the perfect sauce texture. You don't have to blend the sauce though. It looks better, but the lumpy, split buttermilk with the chicken is still delicious. Serve with salad (mine here is cucumber, red onion and parsley, dressed with white wine vinegar and Chicken Salt (page 229), roast potatoes or whatever you feel like.

1 whole chicken (1.2–1.5 kg/
    2 lb 12 oz–3 lb 5 oz)
1½ teaspoons whole black
    peppercorns
400 ml (14 fl oz) buttermilk
6 garlic cloves

Spatchcock the chicken (page 118), then pat dry with paper towel. Place in a bowl or container with the remaining ingredients. Give everything a good mix, cover and allow it to marinate for 4 hours or overnight (a longer marination will give you a juicier, more tender roast chicken).

Preheat the oven to 220°C (430°F).

Place the chicken with all the marinade in a cast iron frying pan or deep roasting tray, skin side up (you should see the chicken skin over the buttermilk mixture so it can crisp up in the oven). Dry the top of the chicken by dabbing it with paper towel, season with a bit of salt, bang it in the oven and roast until the skin is GBD (see page 13) and the chicken hits about 65°C (150°F) at the thickest part, about 30–35 minutes.

Remove the chicken from the buttermilk mixture and allow it to rest for 10–15 minutes (internal temperature will reach up to 70°C/160°F).

Meanwhile, pour the juices from the bottom of the tray (they will look weird but it's okay, trust the process) into a blender and blend until silky smooth.

Cut the chicken however you like and serve with the sauce.

The Best Pizza You Can Make in a Domestic Kitchen

MAKES 1 (FOR 2 PEOPLE) × **ACTIVE TIME 20 MINUTES** × **TOTAL TIME 35 MINUTES**
+ 2 HOURS–OVERNIGHT PROOFING AND 2 HOURS RESTING

I wanted to put this recipe in the book because I feel like we over-romanticise pizza. It feels like the minimal-topping, thin-base Neapolitan pizza has become the pinnacle of pizza, the only pizza that can or should be made. That makes it so complicated for the home cook. Don't get me wrong, Neapolitan pizzas are epic. They're a real art form, but you need so much time, effort and an actual pizza oven to make a good one. The first Neapolitan pizza I threw into the oven was a mess.

The pan pizza we grew up with is the best pizza you can make in a domestic kitchen. It has a thick-ish base, the dough is soft and chewy with a crispy bottom and sides; the edges have that crisped, caramelised, kind of burnt cheese; and it's very heavy on the toppings. It's nostalgic, it's delicious, it's easy, it's what Pizza Hut could have been. Double or triple the recipe for more pizzas and more fun!

PIZZA DOUGH
250 g (9 oz) plain
   (all-purpose) flour
½ teaspoon (2 g) active
   dry yeast
1 teaspoon salt
150 ml (5 fl oz) warm water
1 tablespoon extra virgin olive
   oil, plus extra for greasing

SAUCE
½ × 400 g (14 oz) can
   whole peeled tomatoes
   (San Marzano or whole
   peeled Roma best)
1 garlic clove
¼ teaspoon chilli flakes

TOPPINGS
300 g (10½ oz) pizza cheese
   blend, mozzarella or
   tasty cheese
OPTION 1: hot honey and
   pepperoni
OPTION 2: leftover chicken
   curry garnished with
   Coriander, Mint and
   Yoghurt Chutney
   (page 224) and fresh
   coriander (cilantro) leaves
OPTION 3: whatever you like
Fresh herb leaves

To make the dough, mix the flour, yeast and salt in a bowl. Add the water and oil. Knead until everything comes together nicely, about 5–10 minutes.

Grease a bowl with a little extra oil, then add the dough. Form into a rough ball. Cover the dough in some plastic wrap and, with the seam side of the dough facing down, put it in the fridge to proof overnight. (Overnight will develop the best flavour but if you're short on time, proof it at room temperature until it's doubled in size, around 2–4 hours.)

Grease a cast iron frying pan with a good coating of extra oil, around 1–2 tablespoons. (If you don't have a cast iron pan, a baking tray will do. You'll just have a more square pizza.) Place the dough in the pan. (If you scaled the recipe up for more than one pizza, divide the dough into as many dough balls as you're going to make and lay them out on oiled plates). Oil your fingers and spread the dough. (The dough won't get to the edge of the pan yet.) Cover the pan with a damp tea (dish) towel and rest in a warm environment for 1–2 hours. (To check it's done, try pushing the dough to the edge of the pan. If it doesn't stay, proof for a bit longer.)

Meanwhile, make the sauce by blitzing all the sauce ingredients in a blender until smooth. Adjust the seasoning if you need (go a bit easier on the salt as the toppings can be quite salty).

Preheat the oven to 240°C (465°F).

After the dough has rested, push the dough to the edge of the pan. Top with the sauce, most of the cheese and your toppings option, then the remaining cheese on top. (Make sure you get the cheese to the edge of the dough.) Bake until the cheese is golden brown, about 12–15 minutes.

Take the pizza out and, using a butter knife to get under the edge of the pizza, check the bottom. It should be golden brown and crispy. If it's looking a bit blonde or anaemic, place it on the stove over medium–high heat for 2–3 minutes. Finish by adding fresh herbs.

OG Caramel Slice and a Barfi-Spiced Twist

SERVES 6–10 × ACTIVE TIME 25 MINUTES × TOTAL TIME 55 MINUTES + 4 HOURS SETTING

You go to the bakery, you get a caramel slice. You think it's going to be good, but it rarely is. The ones that are good though — those super gooey, salty ones — they're the best things in the bakery. Those caramel slices are what inspired this recipe. For a few years, I made giant slabs of these and gave out little bits as Christmas gifts for friends and family. My favourite part was the extras I cut for myself. I roughly chopped them and stuck them in the freezer for future sneaky snacks. They're absolutely ridiculous mixed through ice-cream.

BASE
200 g (7 oz) unsalted butter, melted
½ teaspoon vanilla essence
270 g (9½ oz) plain (all-purpose) flour
70 g (2½ oz) desiccated coconut
190 g (6¾ oz) soft brown sugar

CARAMEL
200 g (7 oz) unsalted butter
190 g (6¾ oz) soft brown sugar
2 × 395 g (13¾ oz) cans sweetened condensed milk
FOR OG, ADD:
2 teaspoons vanilla essence
½ teaspoon salt
FOR BARFI-SPICED, ADD:
1 teaspoon vanilla essence
1 teaspoon ground cardamom
¾ fresh nutmeg (3 g), finely grated

CHOCOLATE
200 g (7 oz) milk chocolate, chopped
150 g (5½ oz) dark chocolate, chopped
15 g (½ oz) unsalted butter
FOR BARFI-SPICED, ADD:
10 g (¼ oz) chopped toasted pistachio kernels

Preheat the oven to 180°C (350°F). Line a baking tray (I use a 24 × 34 cm/9½ × 13½ inch tray) with baking paper. (You can put a bit of butter between the paper and the tray to make sure it sticks and doesn't move too much, if you like.)

To make the base, mix the melted butter and vanilla in a bowl. In a separate bowl, mix all the dry ingredients with a good pinch of salt. Mix in the butter mixture. Evenly distribute the mixture over the prepared tray (I find the back of a spoon works best) and bake until lightly golden brown, about 15 minutes.

OPTION 1: OG
To make the caramel, get the butter and sugar in a saucepan over medium heat. Once the butter melts, whisk or stir constantly until it begins to bubble. Keep stirring for about 30–40 seconds, then, while continuing to whisk, add the condensed milk, vanilla and salt. Cook, still stirring, until the mixture becomes golden brown and begins to bubble. As soon as this happens, take off the heat, pour the mixture straight over the base and spread evenly. Put the tray back in the oven for a further 15 minutes. Remove and allow it to cool to room temperature.

OPTION 2: BARFI-SPICED
Do the same as option 1, adding the vanilla, cardamom and nutmeg along with the condensed milk.

Either use a microwave to melt all the chocolate ingredients and a pinch of salt (try 20-second bursts) or use a double boiler (or a heatproof bowl over a saucepan of simmering water, making sure the bowl doesn't touch the water) and gradually heat until everything is melted. Pour on top of the caramel layer (the caramel should be cool before you do this). Sprinkle with pistachio if making the barfi-spiced version.

Let the three-layered sweet chill in the fridge until the chocolate is set, about 4 hours. Slice (see tip) and serve.

TIP Use a hot knife and wipe after every cut to get that perfect straight cut and clean edges.

Victoria Sponge

SERVES 8 × ACTIVE TIME 20 MINUTES × TOTAL TIME 45 MINUTES + 1–2 HOURS COOLING

This cake is one of my family's favourites. It's super simple and classic — gives me *Australian Women's Weekly* vibes.

I'm just going to say it, I made the recipe for the sponge because I'm lazy and baking requires the kind of patience I lack. I wanted one recipe I could use for multiple cakes: this Victoria sponge, Tres Leches (page 204), Lychee and Mango Trifles (page 198) and maybe more in the future. This is it.

Freshly made jam makes all the difference here. It's more liquidy than store bought, so it soaks into the cake. Store-bought jam is also too sickly sweet. This one stays balanced and still tastes like strawberries. Use it as regular jam too, but keep in mind it will be a bit looser than other jams.

5 eggs
200 g (7 oz) caster (superfine)
    sugar, divided evenly
    between 2 bowls
100 ml (3½ fl oz) milk
1 teaspoon vanilla essence
200 g (7 oz) plain (all-purpose)
    flour
1 teaspoon baking powder
¼ teaspoon salt

STRAWBERRY JAM
250 g (9 oz) fresh strawberries
150 g (5½ oz) caster
    (superfine) sugar
1 tablespoon lemon juice
    (from about ½ lemon)

VANILLA CREAM
300 ml (10½ fl oz) thickened
    (whipping) cream
1 teaspoon vanilla bean paste
    or vanilla essence
1 heaped tablespoon (15 g)
    icing (confectioners') sugar,
    plus extra 1 tablespoon

To make the strawberry jam, hull and roughly chop the strawberries. Place 200 g (7 oz) strawberries (reserving the remaining) and the caster sugar in a saucepan over low heat. Bring to a simmer and cook, while stirring periodically, for 20 minutes. At this point the strawberries should be broken down and you'll have a loose jam consistency. Add the lemon juice, reserved strawberries and a small pinch of salt. Simmer for a further 5 minutes. Turn off the heat and allow the jam to cool completely.

Meanwhile, separate the eggs, placing the yolks in one bowl and whites in another. Using a stand mixer or electric beaters, beat the egg whites until frothy, then add about one-third of one sugar bowl and beat until you have soft peaks. Add another third of the sugar from the same bowl and whisk thoroughly. Add the remaining third and whisk until you get stiff peaks.

Preheat the oven to 180°C (360°F). Grease the base (but not the side) of two 15 cm (6 inch) round cake tins, then line the base with baking paper.

To the egg yolks bowl, add the remaining sugar bowl and beat until pale and doubled in size. Pour in the milk and vanilla and beat until combined. Combine all the dry ingredients in a separate bowl, then either sift or very gradually add them to the egg yolk mixture. Beat gently (the low setting on a stand mixer) until just combined. Using a spatula, fold in one-third of the egg white mixture (start by mixing in quickly, then getting progressively gentler). Repeat with the remaining egg white mixture, folding until you create thick ribbons that will hold a figure of eight. Divide the cake mixture between the prepared tins and spread evenly. Bake until a toothpick comes out clean, about 20–25 minutes. Remove and allow the cakes to cool completely in the tins (see tip).

While the cakes cool, make the vanilla cream by placing all the ingredients in a bowl and whisking until you have soft peaks.

To assemble, generously spread just over half of the jam over one of the sponge layers, then top with the vanilla cream. Sandwich with the remaining sponge layer and dust generously with the extra icing sugar.

TIPS To stop the cakes sinking, turn them upside down onto the wire rack to cool in the tins.

If making just one classic sponge (for Tres Leches or Lychee and Mango Trifles), use a rectangular cake tin around 24 x 34 cm (9½ x 13½ inches) and increase the baking time to 25–30 minutes.

Keep the leftover jam in an airtight container in the fridge for up to 2 months.

Sub out the jam with Lemon Curd (page 222) for a twist.

THREE

I GREW UP VERY CONFUSED: MAYBE WE'RE NOT THAT DIFFERENT

The lunches kids would eat at my primary school are something I will always remember. There was this Filipino kid who would bring in rice and these bright red sausages, and eat them with a spoon and fork. There was an Italian kid who would have this epic sandwich with olives in it. Another kid would have a sandwich with butter, tomato sauce and devon. My brother would have potato curry wrapped up in a roti parcel.

Sometimes we'd go to each other's houses for a birthday or something, and I'd experience all these different cultures. Most families had a barbecue but each family would have a different meat on the barbecue, and different sweets and pastries too. I remember going to my Greek friend's barbecue and having grilled halloumi. It was so foreign. We didn't have anything like that in my family. Even though it was just fried cheese with lemon, to me it was amazing. We'd also go to my dad's mates' homes. He had this one Lebanese friend who would invite us over for dinner and cook everything on this little charcoal barbecue. We'd have shish kebabs and tabouli, and Dad would ask 'What's this? How did you make that? What's in the meat?' It was nothing fancy, just our two families in the yard, but the food and way of cooking were totally new to us. Whenever people came to our house, we'd give them a full Indian feast and my parents would tell a story about Fiji. That's how they would connect to people, through food.

I never took roti and curry to school. No one really explained to us what being Fijian-Indian meant. My identity was confusing to me, and my relationship with food was weird. I remember my mate coming over to stay the night and saying my house smelled like curry. I didn't know whether he meant that as a bad thing, but I was embarrassed. I didn't want to be the kid who smelled like curry. I don't know why, but my brother didn't care. He either had balls, or it just never fazed him, but I just wanted to be like the kid with the devon sandwich. I told Mum we had to get devon. She just said, 'Devon? Who's that?' She didn't know what it was so we'd just walk around the supermarket aisles looking for it. When I first took a devon, butter and tomato sauce sandwich to school, I thought it was the coolest thing ever. I ended up having devon sandwiches every single day for a whole year. I grew out of it, but I still never brought a curry to school.

Growing up, Indian was always the least cool culture. I don't know who the marketing director was, but something wasn't working. In movies and on TV the accent was always the punchline of a joke (it is funny, I use it all the time), there were no role models and the food was always the cuisine that gave you the runs. Of course, when you're 15, you never think that, you just feel embarrassed by who you are.

That's not how I feel now.

Weirdly, it started to change with Mexican culture. I was seeing all this Mexican cuisine on cooking shows and YouTube, and it was so cool in a way that Indian food wasn't. Mexican food had this association with parties, good times, laughter and fun, and Indian culture wasn't that at all. Mexican culture also seemed so widely accepted. The chefs on TV weren't Mexican but they were talking about Mexican culture, cooking tacos and drinking tequila. No one was ever making curry. I would never have taken a date to an Indian restaurant, but a Mexican tequila bar? That's sick. Indian culture felt so, so far away from how Mexican was being presented. But the more I got into it, the more I started seeing connections with Indian culture. Mexicans have tortillas and we have roti, they have a sauce called mole which is basically a curry, they have milk desserts and spiced drinks like we do. Mexico and India also both have these ancient cuisines and food is at the centre of all their celebrations. And their celebrations, like ours, are a huge vibe. I thought if I had grown up as a Mexican, I'd still have a mum who cooked with all this chilli and garlic, and I would have taken tacos to school and eaten them at lunchtime with the other kids — but chicken tacos are just the same as roti and curry.

Over time, I came to the conclusion that Indian culture, like Mexican culture, has all these things worth celebrating, just no one was talking about it at that time. That gave me confidence in my own culture, but I was still scared to share that part of me, so I would use Mexican food as a scaffold to present Indian food to other people: here's a tortilla with salsa and charred chicken (really it's a chicken curry with chutney and roti but with a different name). I was giving them Indian flavours but using a language people already associated with cool and attractive things. It was me dealing with my insecurities. I was scared to show people who I was and risk them not accepting me.

But, now it's different. Now when I serve someone Mum's chicken curry and Parti's (Grandma's) chilli chutney, I think I'm giving someone a cool, unique experience. They may not love it (they usually do) but when they eat it, they understand me more. What's crazy to me is just 10 years ago, I never wanted to cook anything I grew up with, but now here you are, reading a book with more than 30 of my family's recipes.

The origins of my family are in South India, but we've been in Fiji for four generations. When they came to Fiji, they found a new environment with new people, new ingredients and a different climate. All the rules of how they used to cook had to adapt and, over generations, they created a new cuisine, Fijian-Indian. To an Indian in India it would be completely rogue — it takes recipes from north, central and south India; it uses Fijian taro and cassava; and soy sauce from the Chinese influence. My family then came to Australia, another new environment with new ingredients, and had to make it up again. Their history is resourcefulness, to use whatever is around you. That is in my DNA and my psyche, and I am 100 per cent inspired by that.

Thanks to where I grew up, I also have a lot of other cultural influences to draw on. My family settled in Western Sydney and when I was a kid we went to steakhouses and Thai restaurants and got Chinese takeaway. Now we go to Korean barbecue, Vietnamese community hubs and Filipino restaurants where everyone speaks Tagalog. If you drive 40 minutes from my house you can get a Fijian cream bun, Islander food and authentic Italian pastries, and on the way, you can have a sausage sandwich at Bunnings. This isn't just happening in restaurants. I'm getting Sri Lankan recipes from my friend's mum, Egyptian food from my neighbour and I'm talking to the dudes at my local coffee shop about how to make French pastries and traditional Chinese food.

Some people don't realise what a culinary hotspot Australia is. And it's getting even better. More people are coming to this country, bringing their food and culture, and everything is mixing and becoming this beautiful mosaic. I am fortunate enough to be a product of that environment and my cooking represents that.

I feel like I can cook anything because that's what I grew up with and that's a part of who I am. It's how I learned to cook, but it's also how I've learned to relate to people and understand others. While I'm now confident to be myself, be Indian and share my family's chicken curry, I also make Filipino sisig, Portuguese-style charcoal chicken and hummus. But maybe other home cooks haven't grown up with that and they don't feel like they can do that. Maybe they feel like they won't do another cuisine justice, or that other cuisines aren't part of who they are.

I can't speak for other cultures, but I'm giving you full permission to cook what I grew up eating. I would love it if you did. Indians might have opinions about what you make but deep down inside our souls, we'll feel accepted and celebrated. So, have my family's chicken curry recipe. Make it like how my family did, or experiment — chuck some Vegemite in it, finish it with oregano or serve it with grilled halloumi and lemon. Go for it. Hopefully, it inspires you to add your own flavour and make your own family chicken curry.

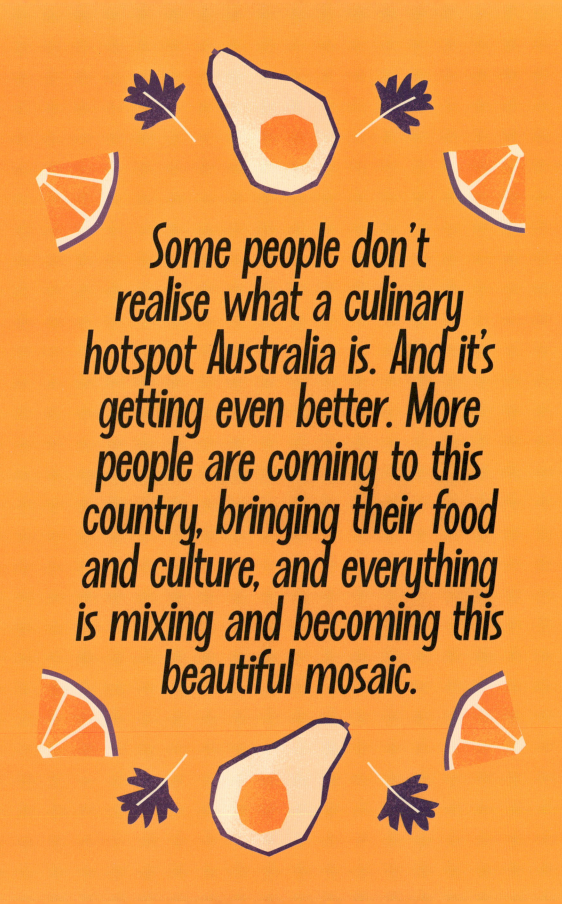

Some people don't realise what a culinary hotspot Australia is. And it's getting even better. More people are coming to this country, bringing their food and culture, and everything is mixing and becoming this beautiful mosaic.

Every great Bollywood film has an over-the-top dramatic song and dance, where the main characters end up unnecessarily wet while remaining fully clothed. So it only felt right for an Australian—Indian cookbook to do the same, and, of course, it had to be at Bondi Beach. Does it make sense? No. Is it necessary? Absolutely not.

Chicken Curry Meets Tacos

This recipe came out of the pressure of the *MasterChef* kitchen. The challenge was to make something creative out of instant noodles. I blitzed the noodles into flour and made tortillas. I took everything you'd find in a chicken curry and blended it with the packet seasoning and marinated the chicken in it. I cooked the chicken until it had a nice char and layered it on a noodle-flour taco with chutney. Chicken curry tacos! I won the challenge and thought, this is actually really good, I should keep this recipe and work on it. This recipe gave me a stepping stone. It wasn't a bold or courageous move, but it was a step in the right direction. When people liked it, really liked it, I thought, why not just give them the authentic chicken curry and see what they think, because that's who I really am.

When I cooked it again, I took more inspiration from Mum's chicken curry for the flavour but kept the grilled chicken from the *MasterChef* recipe. I love that charred, gnarly crust you get and adding the flavour of a curry to that is just a sick combination.

Chicken Curry Tacos with Coriander Green Chilli Chutney

SERVES 4–6 (MAKES 12 TACOS) × ACTIVE TIME 20 MINUTES
TOTAL TIME 30 MINUTES + 2 HOURS–OVERNIGHT MARINATING

6 chicken thighs (about 500 g/
    1 lb 2 oz)

MARINADE
4 garlic cloves
½ brown onion
1 teaspoon caster (superfine) sugar
1 teaspoon ground cumin
1 teaspoon ground turmeric
1½ teaspoons ground coriander
½ teaspoon smoked paprika
½ teaspoon garam masala
1 tablespoon lime juice
    (from about 1 lime)
1½ teaspoons salt, or to taste
100 ml (3½ fl oz) grapeseed oil

PICKLED RADISH
½ cup white vinegar
1 tablespoon caster
    (superfine) sugar
1 tablespoon salt
4 baby radishes, sliced as thin
    as possible (use a mandolin
    to add that finesse)

**CORIANDER AND GREEN
CHILLI CHUTNEY**
1 bunch of fresh coriander
    (cilantro), leaves and stems
    roughly chopped
1–2 jalapeño chillies
1 garlic clove
1 tablespoon lime juice
    (from about 1 lime)
½ teaspoon salt, or to taste
¾ cup (200 g) Greek-style
    yoghurt

TO SERVE
12 × 10–15 cm (4–6 inch) Flour
    Tortillas (page 140)
¼ white or purple cabbage, thinly
    sliced (a mandolin works
    a charm)

Blitz all the marinade ingredients in a blender until smooth, then pour into a bowl. Pat dry the chicken with paper towel, then add to the bowl and massage the marinade into the chicken. Place in the fridge, covered, for 2 hours or overnight to marinate.

Meanwhile, make the pickled radish. Place the vinegar, sugar, salt and ½ cup (125 ml) water in a small saucepan and bring to a simmer while stirring constantly. Once the sugar and salt have dissolved, pour the liquid into a small heatproof bowl or jar. Add the radish, making sure it is completely submerged. Allow it to pickle for 30 minutes or overnight.

To make the chutney, blend all the chutney ingredients, except the yoghurt, in a blender until smooth, then fold in the yoghurt and season with salt to taste.

Heat a barbecue grill plate or a cast iron pan on medium–high. In batches, add the chicken and grill until nicely charred and cooked through, about 3–4 minutes each side. Allow it to rest for 5 minutes, then slice into 1 cm (½ inch) strips.

Heat a frying pan over medium heat, then toast each tortilla until golden, lightly charred and puffed, roughly 30 seconds each side. Wrap the tortillas in a clean tea (dish) towel to keep warm.

Top each tortilla with the cabbage, chicken, chutney and pickled radish and get stuck in.

Chicken Curry Tacos with Coriander Green Chilli Chutney (page 137)

Flour Tortillas

Making your own tortillas is a bit of an effort, but a homemade tortilla will be sturdier, lighter, more flavoursome and more texturally interesting. It also has the structural integrity to handle the fillings and salsas you want to throw on it.

When you have a few people working at it, it's easy. Making a single tortilla takes just over a minute. What I do is make the dough beforehand and when everyone comes over, I get a production line going. One person is rolling, one person is pressing and one person is on the stove cooking and flipping. Everyone is concentrating hard for the first tortilla, but after three or four, we're having fun, chatting and catching up. After you've finished cooking, there's a sense of accomplishment. Your mates have also learnt a new skill. Guarantee, none of my friends have gone home and made tortillas themselves, but they think they can and I think that's important.

1¾ cups (260 g) plain (all-purpose) flour, plus extra for dusting
1 teaspoon baking powder
150 ml (5 fl oz) hot water (boil then let it sit for 5 minutes)
1 tablespoon light olive oil

Mix the flour, baking powder and a generous pinch of salt in a bowl. Pour in the water and oil and mix using a fork (while the water is still hot). Use your hands to knead the dough on a clean work surface until you get a playdough-like consistency, around 5 minutes. Cover with a clean tea (dish) towel and allow the dough to rest for 15 minutes.

Divide the dough into twelve golf ball-sized pieces, about 30 g (1 oz) each. Dust each ball with a little extra flour and roll out to about 2 mm (1⁄16 inch) thick.

Heat a cast iron frying pan or comal pan over high heat. Grab a clean tea (dish) towel to wrap all the finished tortillas in. Place a tortilla in the pan and cook for 10 seconds, flip and cook for a further 30 seconds, then do a final flip and cook for a further 30 seconds (you should see lightly charred spots on each side). Place the tortilla on the tea towel and wrap up so it steams inside. Repeat with the remaining tortillas.

Let all the tortillas sit in the tea towel for 5 minutes to steam through. (The extra cooking inside the tea towel will give you a soft and flexible tortilla.)

Corn Tortillas

MAKES 12 × ACTIVE/TOTAL TIME 20 MINUTES

240 g (8½ oz) masa harina flour (buy online or at specialty grocers)
1 teaspoon salt
280 ml (9½ fl oz) hot water (boil then let it sit for 5 minutes)

Mix the flour and salt in a bowl. Pour in 240 ml (8 fl oz) hot water and mix, first using a fork (while the water is still hot), then your hands. (You want a playdough-like consistency, so add more hot water, if necessary.)

Divide the dough into twelve golf ball-sized pieces, about 40 g (1½ oz) each. Using a sturdy plate with a flat bottom or a tortilla press (lining both with baking paper), press each ball as thin as possible (you're aiming for 2 mm/ ¹⁄₁₆ inch thick).

Heat a cast iron frying pan or comal pan over high heat. Grab a clean tea (dish) towel to wrap all the finished tortillas in. Place a tortilla in the pan and cook for 10 seconds, flip and cook for a further 30 seconds, then do a final flip and cook for a further 30 seconds (you should see lightly charred spots on each side). Place the tortilla on the tea towel and wrap up so it steams inside. Repeat with the remaining tortillas.

Let all the tortillas sit in the tea towel for 5 minutes to steam through. (The extra cooking inside the tea towel will give you a soft and flexible tortilla.)

TIP The stovetop cooking technique for flour tortillas, corn tortillas and roti is the same: cook for 10 seconds, flip, cook for 30 seconds, flip and cook for a final 30 seconds. In the last 30 seconds, they should puff up a bit.

(Queso)
Spicy Cheese Dip

SERVES 4–10 × ACTIVE/TOTAL TIME 10 MINUTES

This is a warm Mexican cheese dip. We need more warm dips out there. You can put this on nachos, in a Philly cheesesteak, in a taco or just enjoy it as a dip with some corn chips.

I use Kraft Singles because they give you that silky, gooey, cheesy texture, which is a result of sodium citrate. You know that cheese sauce liquid lava texture? That's from sodium citrate. Alternatively, you can use other cheeses and add a pinch of sodium citrate and blend it in, but who the heck is buying sodium citrate?

1 tomato, deseeded and
    finely chopped
½ brown onion, finely chopped
1 jalapeño chilli, finely
    chopped
15 g (½ oz) unsalted butter
1 garlic clove, finely chopped
340 ml (11½ fl oz) can
    evaporated milk
250 g (9 oz) cheddar,
    freshly grated
12 slices (216 g packet)
    Kraft Singles

TO SERVE
¼ bunch of fresh coriander
    (cilantro), leaves and stems
    finely chopped
Your favourite corn chips

Combine the tomato, onion and jalapeño in a bowl. Set aside about 2 tablespoons for the garnish.

Heat the butter in a saucepan over medium heat, then add the garlic and remaining tomato-onion-jalapeño mixture and cook for 2–3 minutes until the onion is translucent and soft. Pour in the evaporated milk and, while stirring, gradually add the cheddar and Singles in small batches, only adding more once the cheese has melted in. Continue until all the cheese has been incorporated.

Pour the queso into a serving bowl and top with the coriander and reserved tomato-onion-jalapeño mixture and serve with corn chips.

TIP For killer nachos, layer warm corn chips on a platter with some taco meat from one of my other recipes and smother it in queso. Garnish with the remaining tomato-onion-jalapeño mixture, pickled jalapeño chillies and roughly chopped coriander (cilantro) leaves.

Spicy Black Bean Nachos

SERVES 2–4 × ACTIVE TIME 20 MINUTES × TOTAL TIME 25 MINUTES + 30 MINUTES SOAKING

I don't make this because it's vegan, I make it because it's tasty. It's creamy thanks to the beans, it's kind of cheesy from the nutritional yeast and it's full of protein. It keeps well in the fridge too — up to a week. Take it to work and have it with veggie sticks (like my wife does) or corn chips (like I do).

2 tablespoons grapeseed oil
1 brown onion, finely chopped
2 garlic cloves, thinly sliced
1 teaspoon ground cumin
1 teaspoon smoked paprika
½ teaspoon chilli flakes
420 g (14¾ oz) can black
    beans, rinsed and drained
½ × 400 g (14 oz) can
    diced tomatoes

VEGAN QUESO
½ × 400 g (14 oz) can
    cannellini beans,
    rinsed and drained
½ cup (80 g) cashews,
    soaked in hot water for
    30 minutes and drained
1 garlic clove
Pinch of ground turmeric
Pinch of smoked paprika
2 tablespoons nutritional yeast
½ cup (125 ml) vegetable
    stock, plus extra for
    thinning

TO SERVE
Your favourite corn chips
1 jalapeño chilli (could do
    pickled if you're feeling it,
    see page 144), sliced
½ bunch of fresh coriander
    (cilantro), leaves and stems
    roughly chopped

Heat the grapeseed oil in a cast iron frying pan over medium heat, then add the onion and cook until golden brown, around 3–5 minutes. Add the garlic, cumin, paprika and chilli and cook for another 1 minute. Add the black beans and cook for 1–2 minutes. Add the tomatoes and cook for 2–5 minutes. (It should be a thick saucy consistency by now.) Season with salt and pepper to taste.

To make the vegan queso, blitz all the queso ingredients in a blender until silky smooth. (It should be like a cheese sauce consistency. If you need to thin, add extra stock). Season with salt to taste.

To assemble, briefly warm the corn chips in a 120°C (250°F) oven for 5 minutes or give them a quick 2-minute zap in the microwave. Arrange the warm corn chips on a serving platter, top with the black bean mixture, then the queso. Finish with the sliced jalapeño and coriander.

Charred Corn (Elote)

MAKES 6 × ACTIVE/TOTAL TIME 20 MINUTES + 30 MINUTES–2 HOURS PICKLING

This is a Mexican dish, but it's in the book because of Fiji. When you go to Fiji, you'll see little food stalls on the side of the road doing either fresh coconuts or charred corn. You usually get a choice to have the corn boiled or get it slightly charred over fire and topped with butter, salt and maybe some spices. It's everywhere in Fiji. My dad loves it. When I did my first Juzzy's Taco Pop Up, charred corn had to be on the menu, but I wanted to do a Mexican version with acidity from a lime mayo, a super addictive spice seasoning and feta (which I know isn't traditional, but it is hard to find cotija cheese in Australia) for salty, creamy pops of flavour. People absolutely frothed on it.

6 corncobs, husks on

PICKLED JALAPEÑO
½ cup (125 ml) white vinegar
1 teaspoon salt
½ teaspoon caster (superfine)
    sugar
2–3 jalapeño chillies,
    thinly sliced

LIME MAYO
1 cup (250 ml) Whole Egg
    Mayo (page 226), swapping
    the lemon juice for
    1–2 tablespoons lime juice
    (from about 1–2 limes)
OR
1 cup (250 ml) Whole Egg
    Mayo (page 226)
OR
1 cup (250 ml) your fave
    store-bought mayo mixed
    with 1–2 tablespoons
    lime juice (from about
    1–2 limes)

SEASONING
1 teaspoon ground cumin
1 teaspoon chilli powder
1 teaspoon smoked paprika
1 teaspoon soft brown sugar
1 teaspoon salt

TO SERVE
200 g (7 oz) Greek feta
1 small bunch of fresh
    coriander (cilantro), leaves
    and stems finely chopped

To make the pickled jalapeño, place the vinegar, salt, sugar and ½ cup (125 ml) water in a saucepan. Cook, stirring, over medium heat until the sugar and salt have dissolved. Take off the heat. Place the jalapeño in a heatproof bowl, pour the pickling liquid over the jalapeño and place in the fridge for 30 minutes–2 hours to pickle.

Meanwhile, prepare the lime mayo.

Get a large saucepan of water on the boil over high heat. Peel back the corn husks (leaving intact) and remove any little hairs. Use the husks as a handle to blanch the corn, in batches if necessary, for about 2 minutes. Place the corn over an open flame (gas stove is fine) or grill on the barbecue until charred.

Meanwhile, combine all the seasoning ingredients in a bowl.

Brush the corn generously with the lime mayo, then sprinkle evenly with some of the seasoning. Crumble over the feta and garnish with the pickled jalapeño and coriander.

TIPS To do a salad version of this, follow the recipe but after charring the corn, cut off the kernels and put in a bowl. Dress with the lime mayo and a sprinkle of the seasoning, then top with feta, coriander and pickled jalapeño. I feel like a whole cob of corn looks sick though.

You'll have leftover seasoning. It's great on popcorn or hot chips.

Hummus

Often creaminess is unhealthy, but hummus is creamy healthiness. I love it. As soon as I realised how easy and cheap it is to make, I started making it a lot. The addition of ice cubes gives it a lighter, fluffier texture. Weirdly, I have never had hummus with roti. I don't think I've ever made them at the same time. I always just have pita, but I think it would be just as good with roti.

CLASSIC HUMMUS

1 garlic clove, roughly chopped
2–3 tablespoons extra virgin olive oil
400 g (14 oz) can chickpeas, rinsed and drained
2 tablespoons tahini
2 tablespoons lemon juice (from about 1 lemon), plus extra to taste
1 teaspoon ground cumin
2–3 ice cubes

Place all the ingredients in a food processor with 2–3 tablespoons water. Blitz until silky smooth, about 5 minutes, scraping down the side of the processor halfway through. Taste and adjust with salt and more lemon juice, if it needs it.

GREEN HUMMUS

1 garlic clove, roughly chopped
2–3 tablespoons extra virgin olive oil
400 g (14 oz) can chickpeas, rinsed and drained
2 tablespoons tahini
2 tablespoons lemon juice (from about 1 lemon), plus extra to taste
1 teaspoon ground cumin
1 small bunch of fresh coriander (cilantro), leaves and stems roughly chopped
1–2 long green chillies, roughly chopped
2–3 ice cubes

Place all the ingredients in a food processor with 2–3 tablespoons water. Blitz until silky smooth, about 5 minutes, scraping down the side of the processor halfway through. Taste and adjust with salt and more lemon juice, if it needs it.

TIP For a super tasty salad/side, roast a whole cauliflower or broccoli (or any other brassica) with a bit of salt, pepper and olive oil. Serve on a bed of green hummus and top with toasted almonds. It's epic.

Crispy Lamb Curry with Hummus

SERVES 4–6 × ACTIVE TIME 20 MINUTES × TOTAL TIME 25 MINUTES

This was inspired by something random: dan dan noodles. On top of the noodles, there's crispy pork mince. It's kind of dry but crunchy and adds a lot of texture. I was seeing all these things being put on top of hummus and I thought the crispness of the dan dan mince would be amazing. I wanted to make an Indian-inspired topping with the same texture, so I made this crispy, spiced lamb and got some crunchy, fresh onion and put it over hummus. I like it as a snack or starter with pita or naan, or as a side dish.

1 tablespoon light olive oil
200 g (7 oz) minced
    (ground) lamb
½ teaspoon ground cumin
½ teaspoon garam masala
½ teaspoon chilli powder
¼ teaspoon ground turmeric
4 garlic cloves, crushed
    or 1 tablespoon garlic
    paste (page 59)
400 g (14 oz) Hummus
    (page 145 or store-bought)

SUMAC ONION
½ red onion, thinly sliced
1 tablespoon lemon juice
    (from about ½ lemon)
½ teaspoon sumac

To make the sumac onion, combine all the onion ingredients in a bowl with a pinch of salt. Massage the onion for 1–2 minutes to get all the flavours in there.

Heat the oil in a cast iron pan over medium–high heat, then add the lamb and cook until crispy and GBD (see page 13), about 5–10 minutes. Add all the spices and garlic and cook for another 1–2 minutes. Taste and adjust with salt.

Spread the hummus over the base of a serving bowl and create a well in the middle. Pile in the hot crispy lamb along with all the lamb fat and oil. Top with the sumac onion and enjoy.

TIP Add pomegranate arils for some sweet pops and extra texture.

Green Salad

I went through this phase where I made a lot of monochrome foods. My theory was ingredients that are the same colour pair well together. Out of that hypothesis, and the fact I'm not a big leafy green salad guy (what's the point of those undressed pub side salads?), this salad was born. It's super filling, hearty, interesting and fairly easy and inexpensive to make. It's great as a meal on its own or as a side, and it's one of Esther's most requested dishes.

400 g (14 oz) roasted or
    barbecued veg (see tip)
400 g (14 oz) raw veg (see tip)
20–30 g (¾–1 oz) roasted
    nuts (I like almonds,
    macadamias and peanuts),
    roughly chopped

DRESSING
½ avocado
2 tablespoons lemon juice
    (from about 1 lemon)
¼ bunch of fresh coriander
    (cilantro), leaves and stems
    roughly chopped
¼ bunch of fresh flat-leaf
    parsley, leaves and stems
    roughly chopped
1 green chilli
1 garlic clove, roughly chopped
⅓ cup (80 ml) extra virgin
    olive oil

To make the dressing, blend all the dressing ingredients in a blender until smooth. (You want to get a thick creamy consistency. Add a little water if you need to thin the dressing.) Season with salt and pepper and set aside in the fridge.

Chop the roasted or barbecued veg into random bite-sized pieces. Cut the raw veg into whatever shape you like. (I do a rough chop if it's something like a cucumber. If it's like a long snow pea shape, I'll finely slice or julienne.) Combine all the veg in a big bowl and dress it with the creamy, green dressing. Top with the nuts and eat.

TIP You can use any green vegetables in this (really any vegetable, it just won't look as good). For the roast veg, I like zucchini (courgette) and broccolini because you can get a good char on them. For raw, I like snow peas (mangetout) and cucumber for texture. If you want to add leafy greens you can, but I don't.

Lamb Curry Sausage Rolls

MAKES UP TO 24 × ACTIVE TIME 25 MINUTES × TOTAL TIME 1 HOUR

Mum would make this as a little snack when people came over for tea or for us kids when we came home after school. I don't think she meant for it to taste like curry, but she was always heavy-handed with garlic, onion and spice. So, I just went with it and added more spice to this recipe.

1 tablespoon light olive oil
1 brown onion, finely chopped
3 garlic cloves, crushed or
   finely chopped
1 teaspoon ground cumin
½ teaspoon Fiji masala powder
   or garam masala
½ teaspoon smoked paprika
½ teaspoon chilli flakes
500 g (1 lb 2 oz) minced
   (ground) lamb (see tip)
½ cup (30 g) Japanese (panko)
   breadcrumbs
1 teaspoon salt
1 egg
2 puff pastry sheets,
   thawed if frozen
200 g (7 oz) tasty cheese,
   grated (optional)

EGG WASH
2 tablespoons milk
1 egg

SEASONING
½ teaspoon chilli flakes
½ teaspoon flaky sea salt
½ teaspoon cumin seeds

TO SERVE
Your favourite sauce
   (there are no rules)

Heat the oil in a frying pan over medium heat, then add the onion and garlic and cook until the onion is lightly browned. Add all the powdered spices and chilli and cook for 30 seconds. Transfer the mixture to a bowl and let it cool to room temperature.

Add the lamb, breadcrumbs, salt and egg to the bowl and massage with your hands or a spatula until you have a smooth uniform mixture.

Cut or shape four even rectangles from the puff pastry (if it's store-bought, just cut each sheet in half). Spoon a quarter of the lamb mixture along one side of a pastry rectangle, about 1 cm (½ inch) from the edge. Scatter the cheese over the lamb mixture, if using. Roll up the pastry, starting from the lamb edge, to enclose the filling. Arrange so the seam (where the pastry edges overlap) sits underneath the sausage roll log. Repeat with the remaining pastry and lamb mixture.

Preheat the oven to 180°C (360°F). Line a tray with baking paper.

Meanwhile, slice each log into six even pieces for party size or in half for a meal size, then place the sausage rolls on the prepared tray. Mix the egg wash ingredients in a small bowl until combined. In a separate bowl, combine the seasoning ingredients.

Brush each sausage roll with the egg wash, then sprinkle the seasoning over the top. Bake until the sausage rolls are GBD (see page 13), about 30—35 minutes. Serve with sauce.

TIPS You can swap out the lamb mince for any other kind of mince.

If you want to make these in bulk and freeze them, place the tray in the freezer after rolling. Once frozen solid, transfer to a ziplock bag and store in the freezer for up to 2 months. When you're ready, preheat the oven to 180°C (360°F), egg wash the frozen sausage rolls, season and bake from frozen for 35—40 minutes.

Masala Roast Potatoes

This is my style of cooking: take something nostalgic like potato curry and apply the Western techniques I learned watching cooking shows growing up. You get French-style fluffy-on-the-inside and crispy-on-the-outside potatoes, but with a flavour that's very familiar to me. It's the Hannah Montana philosophy: get the best of both worlds.

I like to serve this with Roast Chicken Curry (page 91) and Chunky Cucumber Raita 'Salad' (page 47). You can also just use it as an alternative to your usual roast potatoes.

1 kg (2 lb 4 oz) potatoes
   (Dutch cream are good),
   peeled if you want (see tip)
3 garlic cloves, thinly sliced
1 bird's eye chilli,
   halved lengthways
1 teaspoon black
   mustard seeds
1 teaspoon ground cumin
½ teaspoon ground turmeric
140 g (5 oz) unsalted butter
   (the best you can find),
   cubed (see tip)
1 tablespoon light olive oil

TO SERVE
1 tablespoon lemon juice
   (from about ½ lemon)
¼ bunch of fresh coriander
   (cilantro), leaves and stems
   finely chopped
Flaky sea salt, to season

Chop the potatoes into quarters, then add to a saucepan of cold, salted water and bring to the boil. Cook until they can easily be pierced by a fork, about 30 minutes. Drain well and allow them to dry, about 5 minutes.

Preheat the oven to 220°C (430°F).

While the potatoes are still hot, add to a bowl with the garlic, chilli, mustard seeds, cumin, turmeric, butter and a pinch of salt. As the butter melts, stir to evenly coat the potatoes. Transfer the spiced potatoes to a roasting tray, and roast, giving them a little mix or toss every 10–15 minutes, until golden brown and crispy, about 30–40 minutes.

To serve, transfer the potatoes to a serving dish, drizzle over the lemon juice, then sprinkle with the coriander and a pinch of flaky sea salt.

TIPS If you can't be bothered to cut and peel the potatoes, just chuck in chat (new) potatoes.

I tried roasting potatoes with all different kinds of fat. Duck fat is good, but my favourite is butter. I friggin' love butter. You're pushing the butter right to the edge with this heat, but it doesn't burn. It just gives great caramelisation and helps get the potatoes crispy.

Mango Habanero Hot Wings

SERVES 2–4 × ACTIVE TIME 25 MINUTES × TOTAL TIME 55 MINUTES

When I first made this with my mate Tyler Fisher, we ate an entire bucket of wings while watching a game of footy. You know when you're eating spicy food, it's as soon as you stop eating you feel the hotness, so we just kept eating. We probably ate 2 kg (4 lb 8 oz) of wings between us. It wasn't sexy, but it was tasty.

Deep-frying wings is good, but it's just so much work. This crispy, oven-baked version is a game changer — I don't know who exactly to credit for the idea but it feels very J. Kenji López-Alt. The baking powder helps with crispness and colour, and the low and slow (to render fat), then high heat (for that crisp) cooking technique gets a very similar result to deep-frying.

1 kg (2 lb 4 oz) chicken wings
1½ tablespoons baking powder
½ teaspoon salt
¼ teaspoon freshly cracked black pepper

HOT SAUCE
1 French shallot, finely chopped
½ carrot, finely chopped
4 garlic cloves, finely chopped
3 habanero chillies, thinly sliced (can do 4 if you're feeling frisky)
1 large mango, roughly chopped
½ cup (125 ml) white vinegar, plus extra to taste
2 teaspoons (10 g) honey, plus extra to taste
1 tablespoon lime juice (from about 1 lime)
15 g (½ oz) cold unsalted butter

Preheat the oven to 150°C (300°F). Lightly grease a wire rack and set over a baking tray (see tip).

Pat dry the chicken wings with paper towel. Place in a bowl and toss with the baking powder, salt and pepper. Transfer to the prepared rack and into the oven for 25 minutes, turning halfway through.

Crank the oven to 230°C (445°F) and continue to bake until golden brown and crisp (again, turning halfway), another 15–20 minutes.

Meanwhile, make the hot sauce. Heat a saucepan over medium heat, then add the shallot, carrot and garlic and cook for 2 minutes to slightly soften the carrots. Add the chilli and cook for another 2 minutes (make sure you have the windows open for this, trust me). Add the mango, then the vinegar, honey, a pinch of salt and a little splash of water (1–2 tablespoons) and bring to a simmer. Cook for 2 minutes, then take off the heat and allow it to cool slightly. Pour the mixture and lime juice into a blender and blitz until silky smooth. Taste and adjust with more salt and extra honey or vinegar if you think it needs it (do whatever tastes good). Divide the sauce in two, pouring one portion into an airtight container and keep in the fridge (see tip).

Place the baked chicken wings in a large bowl. Pour the remaining sauce back into the saucepan and bring to a simmer. Add the cold butter and mix in until melted (the fat will balance the spice and it'll help the sauce cling to the wings). Pour the sauce over the wings and toss, then transfer to a bucket or bowl and boom (literally), time to eat.

TIPS For extra crispy wings, place the wings on the greased rack set over the baking tray in the fridge overnight beforehand to dry out the skin.

Put the leftover hot sauce on whatever you like. I love it over grilled prawns or fish. It will keep in the fridge for up to a month.

Chilli Masala Scrambled Eggs

SERVES 2 × ACTIVE/TOTAL TIME 10 MINUTES

Growing up, Mum often made scrambled eggs for breakfast. I have no idea if it's traditional or if she made it up, but she'd do them with mustard seeds, cumin, chilli, onion and garlic. Technically, from a Western perspective, she'd overcook them, but it gave them caramelisation and a meaty, chewy and juicy texture. She'd then wrap them up in a roti. It's like our eggs on toast. My version takes all the same spices and flavours, but has more decadent, café-style scrambled eggs, which are made with loads of butter — who knew that's what makes café eggs so good.

6 eggs
1 small red onion or French
    shallot, finely chopped
25 g (1 oz) unsalted butter,
    divided into 3 equal chunks
1 long red chilli, finely chopped
2 garlic cloves, finely chopped
½ teaspoon cumin seeds
¼ teaspoon smoked paprika
¼ teaspoon ground turmeric

TO SERVE
2 thick-cut slices of your
    favourite bread
10–20 g (¼–¾ oz) parmesan
½ long red chilli, thinly sliced
¼ bunch of fresh coriander
    (cilantro), leaves and stems
    roughly chopped

Beat the eggs in a bowl with a fork or whisk until combined.

Place the onion or shallot and a chunk of butter in a frying pan over medium heat and cook until the onion is translucent and just beginning to brown. Add the chilli and garlic and cook for 1–2 minutes. Add all the spices and cook until aromatic, about 1 minute. Reduce the heat to low, add the second chunk of butter, then pour in the egg. Instead of stirring, place a spatula underneath the egg, starting from the side of the pan, then gently drag the egg from that side towards the centre. Repeat with different sections of the pan, keeping the egg moving constantly to form small to medium curds. Continue until the egg is almost set (there should be just a small amount of runniness left), then take off the heat. Add the remaining chunk of butter and mix through. Season with salt to taste.

Toast the bread, then top with a generous amount of scrambled egg, a fine grating of parmesan, some chilli and coriander, then get stuck in.

TIP If you have Chilli Chutney (page 218), a quick hack is to whisk 1–2 tablespoons of chutney into the raw eggs (in place of the onion, chilli, garlic and spices), then follow the recipe from the point when you're adding the second chunk of butter and the egg to the pan.

Congee

SERVES 4–6 × ACTIVE TIME 10 MINUTES × TOTAL TIME 1 HOUR

I'm really into cost-effective, big-batch recipes, particularly healthy ones. That's why I've been cooking a lot of congee. I do a big batch, keep it in the fridge and heat it up for breakfast each morning or really anytime I want a quick meal. It's a tiny amount of rice for a huge amount of food, and it's wholesome and healthy. If you make your own stock, it's got protein and collagen in it. It's also an underrated group meal. Invite everyone over for brunch, make congee and put all the toppings on the table and everyone can DIY their own — like a taco night but with congee.

For toppings, I've served it with roasted peanuts, jammy boiled eggs (room-temp egg into boiling water for 7 minutes, then straight into iced water), fresh spring onion (scallion), chilli oil, grilled mushrooms, miso, bacon, leftover roast chicken and chilli oil. Get creative with it.

1 cup (200 or 210 g) jasmine
   or sushi rice
4 cups (1 litre) chicken stock
½ teaspoon MSG or chicken
   stock (bouillon) powder
3 garlic cloves, crushed
   (optional)
10 g (¼ oz) fresh ginger,
   finely grated (optional)

Wash the rice under cold running water until it runs clear. Transfer the rice to a large saucepan along with the stock, MSG or stock powder and 4 cups (1 litre) water. Bring to a rolling simmer, then reduce heat to low and let it tick away, giving it a stir every 15 minutes or so and adding the garlic and ginger (if you've opted in) about 25 minutes in, until the rice has completely softened and you have a watery porridge, about 45 minutes–1 hour.

Grab a whisk and whisk until a thick porridge consistency. Ladle into bowls, top with whatever you're feeling and enjoy.

TIP If you're going to eat the congee on its own, you can do all stock instead of half water half stock. I do half water half stock because, if I'm having lots of toppings, I want it to be light.

Breakfast Tacos ... or Burritos

SERVES 2 (MAKES 6 TACOS OR 2 BURRITOS) × ACTIVE TIME 15 MINUTES
TOTAL TIME 45 MINUTES

You always have leftovers when you make tacos — if you don't have leftovers, proud of you, make extra next time. Usually, the leftovers are the salsa and tortillas, so logically, the next morning you're making more tacos. It's funny how you can just add eggs to something and it somehow becomes an appropriate breakfast. So, scramble some eggs and put it on your taco with whatever else — like potato gems, sausage, leftover salsa — then wrap it all up and there you are, that's a killer breakfast.

150–200 g (5½–7 oz) potato gems or hash browns
2 spicy sausages (chorizo preferably), roughly chopped
4 eggs
6 small tortillas (for tacos) or 2 large tortillas (for burritos)
150 g (5½ oz) whatever cheese you have, shredded

SALSA
4–6 whole canned tomatillos (300–400 g/10½–14 oz)
1 jalapeño chilli
½ avocado
2 teaspoons lime juice (from about ½ lime), plus extra to taste
1 small bunch of fresh coriander (cilantro), leaves and stems roughly chopped
OR
Leftover salsa (any kind) or your favourite hot sauce (my recommendation is El Yucateco Salsa Picante Verde de Chile Habanero)

If you're making the salsa, blend all the salsa ingredients and 1 tablespoon water in a blender until smooth. Season with salt and extra lime juice, if needed.

Cook the gems or hash browns according to packet instructions. Cook the sausage in a frying pan until golden brown, reserving any fat in the pan. Crack the eggs into a bowl and mix with a fork or whisk. Heat the pan back up over medium heat, then pour in the egg. Cook, while mixing constantly, to form a soft scramble. Just before the egg has fully set, take off the heat and hit the eggs with a little pinch of salt and pepper.

OPTION 1: TACOS
Heat a frying pan over medium heat, then toast each small tortilla until golden, lightly charred and puffed, roughly 30 seconds each side. Sprinkle with some cheese and top with the scrambled egg, gems or hash browns and sausage.

OPTION 2: BURRITOS
Divide the scrambled egg among large tortillas, top with some cheese, sausage, gems or hash browns and hot sauce or salsa. Wrap up each burrito, then place in the pan, seam side down, and toast until golden brown, about 1–2 minutes each side.

Hit everything with some more hot sauce or salsa, then enjoy a great breakfast creation.

Fried Fish Sando with Curry Tartare

SERVES 2 × ACTIVE/TOTAL TIME 25 MINUTES

This isn't a family recipe. It's inspired by the Filet-O-Fish, which is the worst item at McDonald's, but I just wanted to know, could you make a better version of a fish sandwich? Yes. A good fish sandwich is killer, one of the most underrated sandwiches there is. It's simple: just good, flaky, juicy fish, shredded lettuce and loads of tartare sauce.

If you're feeling lazy, you can use fish fingers. I don't really have a recommendation for a frozen fish finger, but I'd say Birds Eye and I&J just because their ads were so good. The songs and that wrestling guy were epic. Make the tartare sauce from scratch though. The homemade version is creamier, lighter and all the herbs and pickles give it texture. It makes the sandwich.

½ cup (75 g) plain
(all-purpose) flour
1 egg, lightly beaten
¾ cup (45 g) Japanese (panko)
breadcrumbs
2 fillets of your favourite white,
flaky fish (hake or snapper
work well)
Neutral high smoke point oil,
for deep-frying
Flaky sea salt, to season

TARTARE SAUCE
¼ cup (60 ml) Whole Egg Mayo
(page 226 or store-bought)
1 teaspoon Dijon mustard
30 g (1 oz) gherkins,
roughly chopped
2 tablespoons capers,
rinsed and drained
½ French shallot,
roughly chopped
¼ bunch of fresh dill,
roughly chopped
2 teaspoons lemon juice
(from about ¼ lemon)
1 teaspoon store-bought
chilli paste
½ teaspoon curry powder
1 garlic clove, crushed

TO SERVE
15 g (½ oz) unsalted butter
2 brioche buns, halved
horizontally
¼ iceberg lettuce, shredded
or roughly chopped

To make the tartare sauce, mix together all the sauce ingredients, taste and season with salt.

Get three bowls and place the flour, egg and breadcrumbs in their own bowl. Pat dry the fish with paper towel, then season each side of the fillets with a small pinch of salt and pepper. Dip each fillet in the flour, turning over a few times, until lightly and evenly coated. Douse in the egg, again ensuring it's evenly coated. Finally, place in the breadcrumbs until well covered (this will give you a crunchy texture).

Heat the oil in a cast iron frying pan over medium heat or a deep fryer to 170–180°C (340–360°F). (If you don't have a probe, put a wooden spoon in the oil. If small bubbles appear around the spoon, it's ready.) Line a plate with paper towel.

Gently place the crumbed fish in the pan or deep fryer and fry until golden brown, about 1–2 minutes each side. Drain the finished crumbed fish on the paper towel-lined plate. Hit it with a generous pinch of flaky sea salt.

Heat the butter in a frying pan over medium heat. Toast the cut side of the bun halves until golden brown.

To assemble, spread some tartare sauce over the base of each bun, then layer the lettuce and a piece of fish. Add more tartare sauce on top (as much as your heart desires). Close your sandwich, take a bite and try to remember a time when you had a better fish sandwich.

TIP The tartare sauce will keep in the fridge for up to 1 week. It's also great with the Fiji Fry Fish (page 44).

I grew up having KFC.
It was my family's guilty
pleasure meal when Mum
and Dad didn't want
to cook.

The Holy Trinity of Chicken

I grew up having KFC. It was my family's guilty pleasure meal when Mum and Dad didn't want to cook. That changed when I first had charcoal chicken at a tiny, but legendary, Lebanese chicken shop in Granville, Sydney called El Jannah. It wasn't just the chicken. It was the chips, the Lebanese bread, the pickles and the toum (a garlic sauce you'd have so much of that, even though you'd brush your teeth after, you'd still wake up the next day with garlic breath). When I introduced my family to El Jannah, they loved it. That was it for KFC in my family (well, almost). Charcoal chicken replaced it. El Jannah was one option, the other was Frangos, serving Portuguese-style charcoal chicken. My mates and I were obsessed with both. It became a debate in the group: which one was better?

There's a lot going on with El Jannah chicken. I think it's marinated in olive oil and vinegar, and there's this balance of spices and garlic. I think Frangos is a bit more minimal. They marinate in some kind of fat and probably lemon juice, chilli and herbs. But they're both cooked with similar techniques: slowly over charcoal while being continuously turned. Which one is better? I don't know.

When it was a birthday or celebration, my family or mates would get one of the two. We'd get a big takeaway, take it home and have a feast. One year on my birthday, and I'm not really a birthday guy (I hate celebrating my birthday, I'm working that out), Mum asked me what I wanted. I said, 'KFC, El Jannah and Frangos, the Holy Trinity of chicken.' And we did exactly that, we got them all. It was coordinated with different people getting different chickens, plus chips and sauces from all three, so it would all arrive at the house hot, at the same time. It was the first time we had eaten the trinity together. It was like transcendence, but we were all in the cloud together. It was amazing.

When I moved to Perth I started making charcoal chicken for my mates. They don't have El Jannah there, so their minds were blown — it was like the first time I went to El Jannah. They were having that same moment. I ended up cooking it all the time. It brought people together. We'd always say, 'Let's get together, we'll do something and have chicken.' When I decided to apply for *MasterChef*, I needed a video to show my cooking. I told my mates to come over for State of Origin and chicken. More than 20 people came. I made the El Jannah-inspired recipe (page 166). I thought it would be an epic night, cooking 5–6 chickens, having Lebanese bread, salad, toum and watching the footy, but then NSW lost ... look, I digress but I wanted to say I hate Queensland (sorry/not sorry). So, this spatchcock-style charcoal chicken was what got me into *MasterChef*. Now, it's probably the most common thing I cook today.

'Charcoal' Chicken and Toum

SERVES 4-6 × ACTIVE/TOTAL TIME 45 MINUTES + 2 HOURS-OVERNIGHT MARINATING

For a long time, this was my most cooked recipe. The chicken is insanely flavoursome. It's easy to make in bulk and, importantly, it's super affordable.

In the absence of El Jannah when I moved to Perth, I needed to figure out how to make it. The guy I lived with, Chrishan, worked out the toum. I had to work out the chicken. I did some research and the surprising thing for me was the sourness. You don't notice it when you eat El Jannah, but there is a lot of vinegar or lemon in there, and that's what makes it so juicy and tender.

First, I tried it on the barbecue. The issue was you have to constantly flip the chicken and you end up breaking the skin. At El Jannah they secure the chickens in those grates, holding the skin in place so it can get super crispy. So, I worked out a different method: on the barbecue grill to get the colour and 'charcoal flavour'. It keeps the skin crispy, allows you to do it in bulk and it gets the best result: you get the sear, you get the char, but you also get this gently cooked, super juicy chicken. Even the breast is juicy – it has absorbed so much flavour and moisture in the marinade. At El Jannah, everyone is a thigh and drumstick person, but when I cook it, everyone is a breast person.

I don't know the El Jannah recipe and, to be honest, mine is probably really different. I'd say this goes way harder on the spices, which I did to compensate for the lack of charcoal. If you do know the original El Jannah recipe, shoot me a DM, I'd love to know.

If you don't have a barbecue, there is also an option to just do it in the oven. This is a recipe that really benefits from an overnight marinating, but if you're reading this and want dinner or lunch today, give the marination 2 hours and you'll be good.

1 whole chicken (1.2–1.5 kg/
    2 lb 12 oz–3 lb 5 oz)
Flaky sea salt, to season

MARINADE
⅓ cup (80 ml) light olive oil
2 tablespoons red wine vinegar
2 tablespoons lemon juice
    (from about 1 lemon)
2–3 garlic cloves, crushed, or
    1½ teaspoons garlic paste
    (page 59)
1 teaspoon smoked paprika
1 teaspoon ground cumin
1 teaspoon sumac
1 teaspoon dried
    oregano leaves
½ teaspoon dried thyme
    leaves or 2 sprigs fresh
    thyme, leaves picked
½ teaspoon chilli flakes
½ teaspoon freshly cracked
    black pepper
1 teaspoon salt

Start by spatchcocking the chicken (page 118).

Blitz all the marinade ingredients in a blender until everything is combined. Pat dry the chicken with paper towel, place it in a bowl and cover with the marinade. Give it a little rub down, cover and let it marinate in the fridge for 2 hours or overnight (2 hours does the job, but overnight the chicken absorbs the most flavour and will be slightly more tender from the acid).

Take the chicken out of the fridge and allow it to come to room temperature.

OPTION 1: BARBECUE
Fire up the barbecue to medium. Season each side of the chicken with a light, even coating of flaky sea salt. Once heated, add the chicken, skin side down, to the grill plate and cook until nice and charred, about 10–15 minutes. Flip and cook for a further 10–15 minutes until the chicken is at an internal temperature of 65°C (150°F) at its thickest part. Remove and allow to rest for 15 minutes.

OPTION 2: OVEN
Preheat the oven to 220°C (430°F). Season each side of the chicken with a light, even coating of flaky sea salt. Place the chicken on a baking tray, breast side up, and roast until the chicken is slightly charred and cooked through, about 25 minutes, basting with the juices in the bottom of the tray halfway through (if you can be bothered). Take it out and allow it to rest for 15 minutes.

TOUM

20–25 garlic cloves
½ teaspoon salt
2½ cups (625 ml) canola oil
2 tablespoons lemon juice
(from about 1 lemon)
1 cup (250 ml) Whole Egg
Mayo (optional, page 226
or store-bought; use if you
want a creamier, less
intense toum)

TO SERVE

Salad, pickles, fries and
Lebanese bread (for
an extra good time)

While the chicken is resting, make the toum. Blitz the garlic and salt in a blender until smoothish, then slowly drizzle in the canola oil, alternating with most of the lemon juice. (You should have a light, fluffy toum.) Fold in the mayo here, if using. Season with salt and more of the remaining lemon juice, if necessary.

Break down the chicken however you like. (If you have no idea how, see page 119). Spread a generous amount of toum over a serving plate, place the chicken pieces on top, then drizzle over with any of the resting juices. Serve with a salad, pickles, fries and Lebanese bread.

TIP Make what I call 'chicken toum'. It's a combination of the chicken resting juices from the bottom of the pan and toum. Get them both in a bowl and mix them together. This sauce is the shit. Then you get Lebanese bread, put some salad in the bread, shred some chicken in there too, then drizzle the chicken toum over. It's heavenly.

(Portuguese Chicken)
Frangos Style Chicken

SERVES 4-6 × ACTIVE/TOTAL TIME 45 MINUTES + 2 HOURS-OVERNIGHT MARINATING

Frangos was the original, local charcoal chicken for me. Every time we'd have a meeting for work or church or whatever, we'd end up at the Frangos in Bella Vista, the best charcoal chicken in the Hills (north west Sydney). After many attempts making my own, I discovered a secret ingredient: whisky. A sneaky shot adds aroma and depth to the chicken that you can't get from any other ingredient. Like the El Jannah-inspired recipe, this is really easy to do in bulk, it's affordable and just insanely tasty.

It's kind of a must to serve this with Peri Peri sauce (page 112). Make the sauce ahead of time, then add 2–3 tablespoons of it to your leftover marinade and baste the chicken with it.

There are two ways to cook the chicken: on the barbecue or in the oven.

1 whole chicken (1.2–1.5 kg/
    2 lb 12 oz–3 lb 5 oz)
Flaky sea salt, to season
Peri Peri sauce (page 112),
    to baste (if cooking on the
    barbecue) and to serve

MARINADE
8 garlic cloves, finely chopped
6–10 dried bay leaves,
    ground or blended into
    a fine powder
1 teaspoon smoked paprika
45 ml (1½ fl oz) lemon juice
    (from about 1½ lemons)
40 g (1½ oz) unsalted butter,
    melted
2 tablespoons whisky
1 teaspoon salt

To prepare the chicken, either spatchcock it (page 118) or to get the authentic Portuguese look, do a reverse butterfly by removing the wishbone and cutting through the middle of the breasts, then flipping, breast side up, and pushing the whole chicken flat. Pat dry the chicken with paper towel.

Mix all the marinade ingredients and a few cracks of black pepper in a large bowl. Taste and adjust with salt and pepper. Add the chicken and lovingly massage in the marinade. Cover and place in the fridge to marinate for 2 hours or overnight. (The longer you do it, the juicier and more flavoursome the chicken will be.)

Take the chicken out of the fridge and allow it to come to room temperature.

OPTION 1: BARBECUE
Charcoal is best, but gas does the job. Heat a barbecue grill plate on high. Season each side of the chicken with flaky sea salt, then place the chicken (ideally in a chicken grilling basket, see tip) on the barbecue and grill, flipping every 5–10 minutes, until charred and cooked through, about 20–25 minutes, basting with some Peri Peri sauce halfway through (if you can be bothered). If you're not using a grilling basket just flip one or two times (you don't want to risk breaking up the skin too much). Remove and allow to rest for 15 minutes.

OPTION 2: OVEN
Preheat the oven to 220°C (430°F). Season each side of the chicken with a light, even coating of flaky sea salt. Place the chicken on a baking tray, breast side up, and roast until the chicken is slightly charred and cooked through, about 25 minutes, basting with the juices in the bottom of the tray halfway through (if you can be bothered). Take it out and allow it to rest for 15 minutes.

Serve with Peri Peri sauce.

TIP If you don't have a grilling basket, it's worth investing in one. It takes all the stress out of flipping a chicken or fish.

Jerk Chicken

SERVES 4-6 × ACTIVE/TOTAL TIME 45 MINUTES + 2 HOURS-OVERNIGHT MARINATING

By this point, you can probably tell I'm just obsessed with all different kinds of chicken. Jerk chicken is another recipe I learned through YouTube and TV. You just couldn't get it anywhere in Australia at the time. I didn't have a reference point for what real jerk tasted like, but for me, it was just, is it good and does it taste different to anything I've ever had before? It killed it on both points. Would a Jamaican think it's jerk? I don't know, but I think they'd enjoy it. If they did say it tasted like jerk, it would be the biggest compliment in the world. A tear will come to my eye if that ever happens. If you know what real jerk tastes like and this hits the spot for you, DM me.

1 whole chicken (1.2–1.5 kg/
    2 lb 12 oz–3 lb 5 oz)

MARINADE

2 habanero chillies (if you like
    it spicy go 3 or use scotch
    bonnets if you can find them)
¼ red onion, roughly chopped
4 garlic cloves, roughly chopped
4 spring onions (scallions)
3 tablespoons soy sauce
2 tablespoons apple cider vinegar
2 tablespoons extra virgin olive oil
2½ tablespoons orange
    (from about 1 orange)
1 tablespoon lime juice
    (from about 1 lime)
1 tablespoon freshly grated ginger
    (about 10 g/¼ oz)
2 tablespoons soft brown sugar
1 teaspoon ground nutmeg
1½ teaspoons allspice
1 teaspoon ground cinnamon
1 teaspoon dried thyme leaves

CHARRED PINEAPPLE SALSA

½ pineapple, peeled and
    finely chopped
3 spring onions (scallions)
1 red cayenne chilli,
    finely chopped
1 small bunch of fresh coriander
    (cilantro), leaves and stems
    finely chopped
2 teaspoons lime juice
    (from about ½ lime)
1 tablespoon extra virgin olive oil

Start by spatchcocking the chicken (page 118). Pat dry with paper towel.

Blend all the marinade ingredients and a few cracks of pepper in a blender until smooth. Season with salt to taste. (Warning: it will be hot but don't worry, it will chill out as it cooks.) Place the chicken in a large bowl, then pour over the marinade and massage it in. Place in the fridge, covered, for 2 hours or overnight to marinate. (Overnight will give you a juicier and more flavoursome chicken.)

Take the chicken out of the fridge and allow it to come to room temperature.

Fire up the barbecue to medium, then throw the chicken on the grill plate, reserving the excess marinade left in the bowl. Cook, covered, until the chicken is cooked through, about 10–15 minutes each side, basting with the reserved marinade. While you're cooking, be careful not to burn the marinade. (If you're worried, turn down the heat or remove the chicken for a bit.) Remove and allow to rest for 10–15 minutes.

While you're cooking the chicken, make the salsa. Get the pineapple and spring onion on the barbecue and grill until they've got a bit of char on both sides. Finely chop both, then add to a bowl along with the cayenne chilli and coriander. Dress with the lime juice, extra virgin olive oil and salt to taste.

Break down the chicken however you like (see page 119 for tips). Arrange on a serving plate, top with a generous amount of salsa and serve.

Masala Sweet Potato Tacos

SERVES 4-6 (MAKES 20 TACOS) × **ACTIVE TIME 20 MINUTES** × **TOTAL TIME 1 HOUR**

If you're having a taco night and you could only serve one taco — no idea why you would do that, but if you did — this should be that taco. The texture shouldn't make sense; everything is soft, but it feels so luxurious and just melts together as you eat it. I call it the silent assassin of tacos because no one goes for it first, but everyone goes for seconds. It's super affordable too. You can make a lot of these very cheaply.

500 g (1 lb 2 oz) sweet potato
100 g (3½ oz) unsalted butter,
    melted
1 teaspoon ground cumin
1 teaspoon smoked paprika
1 teaspoon chilli powder
1 teaspoon garam masala

SALSA ROJA
2 tomatoes
½ brown onion
1 jalapeño chilli
1 garlic clove
1 small bunch of fresh
    coriander (cilantro),
    leaves and stems
1 tablespoon lime juice
    (from about 1 lime)

**CRISPY SWEET POTATO
SKINS (OPTIONAL)**
Neutral high smoke point oil,
    for deep-frying
1 tablespoon chickpea
    flour (besan) (cornflour/
    cornstarch or fine rice flour
    works too)

TO SERVE
20 × 10–15 cm (4–6 inch)
    Flour or Corn Tortillas
    (page 140–141)
100 g (3½ oz) Greek feta,
    crumbled
¼ brown onion, finely chopped
¼ bunch of fresh coriander
    (cilantro), leaves and stems
    roughly chopped
Lime wedges

Preheat the oven to 200°C (400°F).

Peel the sweet potato, saving the skin for the crispy sweet potato skins, if you're making them. Cut the sweet potato into 2–3 cm (¾–1¼ inch) cubes and transfer to a baking tray. Pour the butter over the sweet potato, then add the powdered spices and a pinch of salt. Give it a good mix. Roast for 15 minutes, then turn and roast until soft and nicely caramelised, another 15–25 minutes.

While the sweet potato is in the oven, make the salsa roja. Roughly chop the tomato, onion, jalapeño, garlic and coriander, then pulse in a food processor until you get something halfway between a fine chop and a chunky relish. Season with the lime juice and salt to taste.

If you're making the crispy sweet potato skins, heat the oil in a cast iron frying pan over medium heat or a deep fryer to 170–180°C (340–360°F). (If you don't have a probe, put a wooden spoon in the oil. If small bubbles appear around the spoon, it's ready.) Line a plate with paper towel.

Julienne the reserved sweet potato skins (or thinly slice into matchsticks). Coat in the flour. Fry the sweet potato skins, in batches, until golden brown and crispy, then drain on the paper towel-lined plate. Hit them with a pinch of salt.

Heat a frying pan over medium heat, then toast each tortilla until golden, lightly charred and puffed, roughly 30 seconds each side. Wrap the tortillas in a clean tea (dish) towel to keep warm.

Top the tortillas with the sweet potato filling and salsa. Sprinkle with the feta, raw onion, crispy potato skins, if using, and coriander. Serve with lime wedges to squeeze over.

TIP If you want a next-level salsa, char all the veggies on the barbecue or under the oven grill before you blend them. You'll get a nice smoky flavour.

As pictured on pages 174–175

Pork Tacos

**SERVES 4–6 (MAKES 20 TACOS) × ACTIVE/TOTAL TIME 25 MINUTES
+ 15 MINUTES SOAKING AND 2 HOURS–OVERNIGHT MARINATING**

Tacos al pastor is one of the most iconic street food tacos. Traditionally, they're made with super thinly sliced pork, stacked and cooked on a vertical spit like a doner kebab.

Technically this isn't it — if it's not cooked on the spit, it's not tacos al pastor. But, let's be honest, who has a spit, so I'm calling this tacos al pastor. The flavour is close to the real deal and anyone can do this version. It's epic for a summer barbecue; the chargrilled pineapple and the smokiness you get from the pork really make it.

1.5–2 kg (3 lb 5 oz–4 lb 8 oz)
  boneless pork shoulder
1 pineapple, peeled and cut
  into 2 cm (¾ inch) slices

MARINADE
5 dried guajillo chillies
4 dried ancho chillies
2 dried morita chillies
50 g (1¾ oz) achiote paste
8 garlic cloves
1 teaspoon dried Mexican
  oregano leaves (regular
  dried oregano leaves
  work too)
100 ml (3½ fl oz) white vinegar
240 ml (8 fl oz) pineapple juice
  (it's a lot of work to juice,
  I recommend buying it)
1 tablespoon lime juice
  (from about 1 lime)
1 tablespoon soft brown sugar
2 teaspoons ground cumin
1 tablespoon salt

TO SERVE
1 brown onion, finely chopped
1 bunch of fresh coriander
  (cilantro), leaves and stems
  finely chopped
20 × 10–15 cm (4–6 inch)
  Flour Tortillas (page 140)

To make the marinade, remove and discard the seeds from the dried chillies, then soak them in hot water for 10–15 minutes to rehydrate and soften. Take the chillies out of the water and blitz in a blender with the remaining marinade ingredients until smooth.

Pat dry the pork with paper towel, then cut into 1 cm (½ inch) thick slices. Place in a bowl. Cover with the marinade and place, covered, in the fridge to marinate, ideally overnight (but you can get away with 2 hours).

Heat a barbecue grill plate or cast iron frying pan on high. Add the pineapple and cook until charred and caramelised, around 2–4 minutes each side. Remove and roughly chop into small cubes. Cook the pork until it's nicely golden brown with some slight char, around 1–2 minutes each side. Allow it to rest, then chop into bite-sized pieces.

For the garnish, mix the onion and coriander in a bowl.

Heat a frying pan over medium heat, then toast each tortilla until golden, lightly charred and puffed, roughly 30 seconds each side. Wrap the tortillas in a clean tea (dish) towel to keep warm.

You can assemble each taco or your guests can DIY. Top with a generous mound of pork, pineapple and a sprinkle of the garnish, then get it in your gob.

TIPS Get the dried chillies and achiote paste online or at specialty grocers.

I think charred pineapple is the superior way to eat the fruit. Grill some pineapple, dice it up and serve it with vanilla ice-cream and rum syrup (heat 1:1 rum to sugar until the sugar melts, then let it cool).

Clockwise from top left: Lamb Birria Tacos (page 176), Masala Sweet potato tacos (page 172), and Steak Tacos (page 178)

Lamb Birria Tacos

If you've never had a birria taco, it's a super juicy, cheesy, crispy taco with what I'd say is a curry-like broth or consommé.

Getting the chillies is annoying, but once you buy them you have a pantry staple for good. I think the ancho is the most important chilli in the mix. It has this paprika sweetness and it adds colour. The guajillo gives smokiness, the morita adds spiciness and a savoury smokiness, and the de árbol has heaps of colour and spice. The combination of all of these gives you a flavour you can't replicate.

4 dried guajillo chillies
2 dried ancho chillies
2 dried morita chillies
2 dried chile de árbol chillies
1 deboned lamb shoulder
(1.5–2 kg/3 lb 5 oz–
4 lb 8 oz)
1 tablespoon light olive oil
1 brown onion, roughly
chopped
4 garlic cloves, roughly
chopped
2 tomatoes, roughly chopped
4 cups (1 litre) chicken stock
2 tablespoons apple
cider vinegar
1 teaspoon ground cumin
1 teaspoon dried oregano
leaves

Roughly chop and deseed all the dried chillies. (If you want it really spicy, keep the seeds in.)

Preheat the oven to 160°C (320°F).

Cut the lamb into 3–4 cm (1¼–1½ inch) chunks and season with a good pinch of salt. Heat the oil in a Dutch oven or ovenproof saucepan over high heat, then sear the lamb, in batches, until golden brown, about 2–3 minutes each side. Remove and set aside on a plate.

Add the onion, garlic and all the chillies to the pan and cook until you get a bit of browning on the onion. Add the tomato, stock and vinegar and bring to a simmer. Simmer until the chillies have softened, about 5–10 minutes, then add the cumin and oregano.

Using a stick blender, blend until smooth. (If you don't have a stick blender, add to a regular blender in batches.) Return the mixture and all the lamb to the pan. (If the lamb isn't covered by the liquid, top up with water.) Pop the lid on and place in the oven for 2½ hours or until the lamb easily falls apart with the twist of a fork.

Remove the lamb from the pan (make sure to keep the broth) and pull it apart using two forks or, if you can handle the heat, your hands. Transfer to a bowl. Taste the broth and season with salt if it needs it, then add a little of the broth to the lamb to keep it moist.

TO SERVE
20 × 10–15 cm (4–6 inch)
    Corn Tortillas (page 141)
250 g (9 oz) mozzarella,
    grated or shredded
½ brown onion, finely chopped
1 small bunch of fresh
    coriander (cilantro), leaves
    and stems roughly chopped
Margaritas (optional,
    page 208)

Now, build the tacos. Heat a cast iron frying pan over medium heat. Dip one side of a tortilla in the broth (skim the top, where the fat is, rather than plunging it in), then transfer the tortilla to the hot pan, wet side down. While the tortilla is frying for 30–45 seconds, add some shredded lamb and mozzarella on top. Fold in half, then flip and cook until the tortilla is slightly crispy and the cheese is melted. Open up the tortilla slightly and throw in some of the raw onion and coriander. Depending on the size of the frying pan, you can fry 3–4 tortillas at once and get a production line going. Repeat with the remaining tortillas, lamb, mozzarella, raw onion and coriander.

Serve with a bowl of the broth and, if you're so inclined, margaritas.

TIPS A little twist you can do: dip a tortilla in the broth, char on one side, then as you flip, scatter cheese into the frying pan so the flipped tortilla will land on the cheese. Then, while the cheese is getting crispy, fill the taco, so when you invert it, crispy cheese will be on the outside.

You can find Mexican ingredients online easily, and they're becoming more common at fancy grocery stores too.

These dried chillies have a great shelf life. Use them to make hot sauce. Toast, deseed and soak the chillies in hot water to soften. Drain, then blend with white vinegar (about half the weight of the chillies) or whatever you want in your sauce. Or make Mexican Chilli Oil (page 231).

Steak Tacos

(Carne Asada Tacos)

**SERVES 4–6 (MAKES 20 TACOS) × ACTIVE/TOTAL TIME 20 MINUTES
+ 2 HOURS–OVERNIGHT MARINATING**

When I was getting into Mexican food, there weren't that many Mexican restaurants around. My experience was the Mad Mex and Guzman y Gomez chains. A lot of my Mexican recipes have come from me wanting to try something I've seen on TV or YouTube, but not having anywhere to eat it. This is one of those recipes.

It's just four things: tortilla, marinated steak, tomatillo salsa and raw onion. If you've never had a tomatillo, imagine tomato without any of the sweetness or acidity. It gives the salsa a deeply savoury flavour.

500–600 g (1 lb 2 oz–
  1 lb 5 oz) skirt steak

MARINADE
50 ml (1½ fl oz) orange juice
  (from about 1 orange)
1 tablespoon lime juice
  (from about 1 lime)
1½ teaspoons ground cumin
1 tablespoon soy sauce
4 garlic cloves, thinly sliced
1 jalapeño chilli, thinly sliced
1 teaspoon caster (superfine)
  sugar
1 teaspoon salt

TOMATILLO SALSA
4 whole canned tomatillos
  (300 g/10½ oz)
1 jalapeño chilli
¼ brown onion
1 garlic clove
Light olive oil, for drizzling
1 tablespoon lime juice
  (from about 1 lime),
  plus extra to taste
1 small bunch of fresh
  coriander (cilantro),
  leaves and stems
½ avocado (optional: if you
  want extra creaminess,
  see tip)

TO SERVE
20 × 10–15 cm (4–6 inch)
  Flour Tortillas (page 140)
¼ brown onion, finely chopped
1 small bunch of fresh
  coriander (cilantro), leaves
  and stems finely chopped

Mix all the marinade ingredients in a bowl. Pat dry the steak with paper towel, then add the steak to the bowl and coat in the marinade. Cover and place in the fridge to marinate for a minimum of 2 hours, but overnight is best. (The longer you can marinate the meat the better. The meat will absorb all the flavour and the citrus will transform the meat, making it tender.)

Meanwhile, make the salsa. Fire up the barbecue to high (or preheat the oven grill to its highest temperature). Drizzle the tomatillos, chilli, onion and garlic with oil. (If using the oven grill, transfer the mixture to a baking tray.) Grill the veggies until everything starts to char, then transfer to a blender. Add the lime juice, coriander and avocado, if using. Pulse until everything is evenly chopped. Taste and season with salt and extra lime juice, if necessary. (It should be savoury, bright and acidic with a little sweetness and a good hum of spice.)

Take the steak out of the fridge and allow it to come to room temperature.

Fire up the barbecue grill plate (if you haven't already) or a cast iron frying pan to high until it's smoking. Cook the steak for about 2 minutes each side for medium–medium/rare (do the steak done test on pages 107–108 for more accurate timings). Allow the steak to rest for 2–5 minutes, then slice across the grain into small, bite-sized pieces.

Heat a frying pan over medium heat, then toast each tortilla until golden, lightly charred and puffed, roughly 30 seconds each side. Wrap the tortillas in a clean tea (dish) towel to keep warm.

Place a generous amount of steak on each tortilla. Top with the tomatillo salsa and a sprinkle of raw onion and coriander.

TIPS Put the avocado in the salsa to give it a creamy texture.

You'll have leftover salsa, but you can use it on anything. I have it the next day on corn chips or eggs.

As pictured on pages 174–175

Sizzling Pork Sisig

SERVES 4-6 × ACTIVE/TOTAL TIME 30 MINUTES + 1 HOUR-OVERNIGHT SOAKING

I first had this dish at a Filipino restaurant in Blacktown. Esther and I took my family out and, for me, this was the best thing we ate. I tried telling Esther's mum and Lola (her grandma on her Filipino side) about it, thinking it would be a cool way to connect with them, but they had no idea what it was. Turns out it's more of a modern dish you usually have with beer. It's perfect for that — crispy, chewy, salty, spicy and a bit of lemon makes it bright and acidic too.

Traditionally, it's made with pig head, using all the gelatinous bits from the ear and cheek, but this version (same as the one we had in Blacktown) is made with leftover lechon (Filipino roast suckling pig). I love the idea of turning leftovers into a new dish. Roast pork often isn't as good the next day, because you lose the texture from the crackling, but this is an amazing way to give it a second life.

100 g (3½ oz) chicken livers
(see tip)
1 cup (250 ml) milk
400 g (14 oz) leftover
Roast Crispy Pork Belly
(page 116), roughly
chopped into 1 cm (½ inch)
pieces, or raw pork belly,
rind removed, meat cut into
1–2 cm (½–¾ inch) strips
1–2 tablespoons canola oil
1 red onion, finely chopped
3 garlic cloves, thinly sliced
2 bird's eye chillies,
thinly sliced
15 g (½ oz) unsalted butter
2 tablespoons soy sauce
1 tablespoon lemon juice
(from about ½ lemon)
1 egg

TO SERVE
Jasmine rice
½ lemon, cut into wedges

Pat dry the livers with a paper towel, then place in a bowl with the milk and leave in the fridge for 1 hour or overnight to soak.

If using raw pork belly, place in a bowl with 1 tablespoon oil, a pinch of salt and a few cracks of black pepper and mix to coat. Heat a cast iron frying pan over medium heat, then cook the pork until deeply golden brown, about 4–5 minutes each side. Remove from the pan and rest for 5 minutes. Roughly chop into 1 cm (½ inch) pieces.

Remove the livers from the milk, pat dry with paper towel and set aside. Heat the remaining tablespoon of oil in the pan over medium–high heat, then add the onion (reserving a small handful for garnish) and cook for 2 minutes. Add the livers, garlic, half the chilli and a good pinch of salt and pepper. Cook until the livers are golden brown, about 5 minutes. Transfer the mixture to a bowl. Rest for 5 minutes. Finely chop the livers and return to the bowl. Mix in the pork. (This is the sisig mixture.)

Just before you're ready to serve (table set, guests waiting, hot steamy jasmine rice ready to go and a board on the table for the hot pan that's to come), heat the butter in a cast iron frying pan over medium heat, then add the sisig mixture, soy sauce and lemon juice. Mix everything together, taste and adjust with salt. Create a little space in the middle of the pan and crack an egg into the centre, then sprinkle the reserved onion and remaining chilli over the top. When the egg white is set, take the pan off the heat and serve, garnishing with the lemon wedges.

TIP You don't have to use the livers, but they give more depth of flavour and a more interesting texture, like a pâté-style paste that brings everything together. Soaking them in milk softens the flavour. Otherwise, they can be a bit bitter and metallic.

You'd never do this in an Indian kitchen, but this way of cooking is just easier.

Slow Roast Lamb 'Curry' with Mint Rice

**SERVES 4–6 × ACTIVE TIME 20 MINUTES × TOTAL TIME 3 HOURS 30 MINUTES
+ 2 HOURS–OVERNIGHT MARINATING**

Serving a whole lamb shoulder at the table is always a special moment; it's a bit of theatre at dinner. If you're Greek, you've probably had that experience many times, but we never ate lamb shoulder. I'd see it in restaurants and on TV, and I wanted to experiment with the same amazing cut, but with the spices and flavours of an Indian lamb curry. As lamb is quite gamey, it can take a lot of spice.

To be honest, this recipe came from laziness. It's easy: just marinate the day before everyone comes over, then on the day, put it in the oven, cook rice and the prep is done. Go hang out with friends for two to three hours then, after you've finished that last game of Catan, dinner is ready. I'm busy, everyone is. Make it easy.

The mint rice adds freshness and texture. Plus, mint and lamb is such a classic combo. If you want to pimp it up even more, serve it with some chilli chutney and pickles. Get it all in there.

1 lamb shoulder (1.5–2 kg/
 3 lb 5 oz–4 lb 8 oz)
400 g (14 oz) can diced
 tomatoes

MARINADE
10 g (¼ oz) fresh ginger, finely
 grated, or 1 teaspoon
 ginger paste (page 59)
8–9 garlic cloves, crushed,
 or 1¼ tablespoons garlic
 paste (page 59)
1½ teaspoons smoked paprika
1 teaspoon chilli flakes
2 teaspoons flaky sea salt
1 teaspoon ground turmeric
1 teaspoon ground coriander
2 teaspoons ground cumin
1 tablespoon lemon juice
 (from about ½ lemon)
⅓ cup (80 ml) light olive oil

MINT RICE
1 cup (200 g) basmati rice
1 tablespoon lemon juice
 (from about ½ lemon)
100 g (3½ oz) roast slivered
 almonds
1 bunch of fresh mint,
 leaves picked

TO SERVE
1 small bunch of fresh
 coriander (cilantro),
 leaves picked
Flaky sea salt, to season

Place all the marinade ingredients in a large bowl and mix well. Pat dry the lamb with paper towel, then place in the bowl and massage in the marinade. Allow it to marinate in the fridge for 2 hours or overnight (the longer the better the flavour and texture).

Preheat the oven to 160°C (320°F).

In a deep baking tray, add the tomatoes, then half-fill the can with water (I always like to fill the empty tomato can with water to get every last ounce of tomato) and pour into the tray. Place the lamb on the tray and tightly cover with baking paper, then foil. Roast until the lamb falls apart with the prod of a fork, about 3 hours.

Take out the lamb and crank the oven to 250°C (480°F). Remove the foil and baking paper, then put the tray back in the oven and roast until nicely charred and caramelised, about 15–20 minutes. Allow the lamb to rest for 15–20 minutes.

Meanwhile, make the mint rice. Cook the rice according to page 28, then pour over the lemon juice, add the almonds and mint and mix.

Pour any of the rich tomato sauce from the lamb tray into a jug. Bring the lamb to the dining table, family style, and shred with tongs or two forks. Pour the tomato sauce over the shredded lamb and garnish with fresh coriander and flaky sea salt. Serve with the mint rice and enjoy.

Slow Roast Lamb 'Curry' with Mint Rice (page 181)

Butter Roasted Seafood

SERVES 4–6 × ACTIVE TIME 5 MINUTES × TOTAL TIME 10 MINUTES

A whole fish roasted with butter will caramelise super hard. The butter gets a perfect beurre noisette; not burnt but it's got character and depth to it. The Curry Leaf or Chilli Chutney Compound Butters (page 230) will just perfume it all. And it's so easy. I do all the prep in 5 minutes.

800 g–1 kg (1 lb 12 oz–
2 lb 4 oz) whole fish (such
as flounder, Murray cod,
coral trout or snapper),
scaled and gutted, or
800 g (1 lb 12 oz) prawns
(about 12 large prawns)
100–150 g (3½–5½ oz)
Compound Butter of choice
(page 230), softened

TO SERVE
1 tablespoon lemon juice
(from about ½ lemon)
Flaky sea salt, to season

Preheat the oven grill to 250°C (480°F).

OPTION 1: WHOLE FISH
Pat dry the fish with paper towel, then score the top of the fish with a few deep cuts (they should go to the bone). Spread 2–3 tablespoons compound butter over the base of a cast iron frying pan. Place the fish on top. Spread another 2–3 tablespoons compound butter over the fish and into the cuts. Place the pan under the grill until the fish is charred and cooked through, about 7 minutes.

OPTION 2: PRAWNS
Leaving the prawn heads on, gut and butterfly or half shell (use scissors to remove the shell on one side of each prawn by cutting along the back and between the legs). Place on a baking tray or ovenproof frying pan. Top with 2–3 tablespoons compound butter, then place under the grill until the prawns are charred and cooked through, about 5 minutes.

To serve, place the fish or prawns on a serving platter and pour over any remaining butter from the pan or tray, hit with the lemon juice and a good pinch of flaky sea salt.

TIPS You can use any seafood here. I like flounder and prawns. It would be stunning with crab or lobster too. It's also great with roast chicken.

Instead of roasting under the oven grill, you can pan-fry the fish, prawns or chicken in a cast iron frying pan and either baste or finish with a few tablespoons of compound butter.

Curry Mussels

SERVES 4 × ACTIVE/TOTAL TIME 15 MINUTES

I didn't grow up eating mussel curry, but I love mussels. They're delicious and, for seafood, they're very affordable and sustainable. We should be eating more of them. You know that spicy tomato mussel dish you get in Italian restaurants? A glass of white wine, baguette, big bowl of mussels, great vibe — this is the curry version of that. It's best eaten out of a big communal bowl or pot with your hands.

1 kg (2 lb 4 oz) mussels, shells on
1 tablespoon light olive oil
1 French shallot, finely chopped
3 garlic cloves, thinly sliced
15 g (½ oz) fresh ginger, finely chopped
1 long red chilli, sliced
1 teaspoon The Mixture (page 60) or ¼ teaspoon each of cumin seeds and black mustard seeds, and ⅛ teaspoon fenugreek seeds
½ teaspoon ground turmeric
½ teaspoon Fiji masala powder or garam masala
½ teaspoon ground cumin
½ teaspoon chilli powder
1 teaspoon ground coriander
200 ml (7 fl oz) coconut cream
2 teaspoons lime juice (from about ½ lime)

TO SERVE
1 small bunch of fresh coriander (cilantro), leaves picked
Crusty baguette or Rice (page 28)

Wash the mussels and remove the beards.

Heat the oil in a large saucepan over medium heat, then add the shallot, garlic, ginger, fresh chilli and whole spices. Cook until the shallot starts to turn golden brown, about 2–3 minutes. Add the powdered spices and toast for 30 seconds. Add the coconut cream, bring to a simmer, then add the mussels. Cover and cook until all the mussels open, about 5–7 minutes. Taste and season with the lime juice and salt.

Pour everything into a large serving bowl, garnish with the fresh coriander and serve with crusty baguette or rice.

Masala Roast Spanish Mackerel with an Indian-ish Chimichurri-ish Sauce

SERVES 4–6 × ACTIVE TIME 20 MINUTES × TOTAL TIME 30 MINUTES + 30 MINUTES–4 HOURS MARINATING

Usually, when we had mackerel growing up, it would be in a curry or deep-fried. I wanted to do a healthier, fresher take. The Indian-ish chimichurri is just a classic chimichurri with extra garlic, chilli and a bit of cumin. The chimichurri gets to know the fish juices, and you get a really savoury, fresh and delicious flavour.

500–600 g (1 lb 2 oz–
    1 lb 5 oz) Spanish mackerel
    cutlets, cut into 2 cm
    (¾ inch) thick cutlets with
    the bones in (see tip)
Neutral high smoke point oil,
    for frying (if using oven
    method)

MARINADE
½ teaspoon ground cumin
½ teaspoon ground coriander
½ teaspoon ground turmeric
½ teaspoon chilli powder
1 tablespoon extra virgin
    olive oil

INDIAN-ISH CHIMICHURRI
2 garlic cloves
1 French shallot
1 bird's eye chilli
1 small bunch of fresh flat-leaf
    parsley, leaves and stems
1 small bunch of fresh
    coriander (cilantro), leaves
    and stems
¼ cup (60 ml) extra virgin
    olive oil
2 teaspoons lime juice
    (from about ½ lime)
½ teaspoon ground cumin

TO SERVE
Lemon wedges
Masala Roast Potatoes
    (page 153) and Coconut
    Buns (page 53)

Pat dry the fish with paper towel. Place in a bowl with all the marinade ingredients, a good pinch of salt and a few cracks of black pepper. Let them sit, covered, in the fridge, for 30 minutes–4 hours to marinate.

To make the chimichurri, either thinly slice all the fresh ingredients as best you can and combine with the oil, lime juice and cumin, or roughly chop the fresh ingredients and throw them into a food processor with everything else and pulse. (Chopping will give you the better sauce, but it takes 2–5 minutes.) Season with salt and a few cracks of black pepper to taste.

OPTION 1: OVEN
Preheat the oven grill to 250°C (480°F). Drizzle some neutral oil into a cast iron frying pan, then add the fish. Cook for 5 minutes each side (you should get a good char on both sides and the fish should be cooked through).

OPTION 2: BARBECUE
Preheat a barbecue to high. Cook the fish for 4–6 minutes each side (you should get a good char on both sides and the fish should be cooked through).

Allow the fish to rest for 3 minutes, then arrange on a serving platter. Generously dress each piece with the chimichurri and let sit for 1–2 minutes so the fish resting juices and chimi become one.

Serve with lemon wedges, masala roast potatoes and coconut buns.

TIP Spanish Mackerel freezes and thaws great. I always get a little extra to stash in the freezer.

What to Make When You Can't Be Bothered Making Anything

You know that discussion you have when you're hungry and it's 6pm?

Me: Babe, what do you feel like for dinner?

Esther: I don't know. You choose.

Me: Do you want to go out? Should I cook or do you want to cook?

The answer is mostly no, but I still ask.

Esther: We can go out, unless you want to cook?

Me: Can't be bothered cooking. Where do you want to go?

Esther: I don't know. You choose.

Me: Pizza?

Esther: No.

We both look at our phones for options.

Me: Burgers?

Esther: Depends, how far?

I do the maths and realise it will take 20 minutes to get there, 5 minutes to park and 10 minutes before we get our meal. At best it's 30—40 minutes until we eat. I look at the time, it's now 6.30pm. I'm starving and Esther is getting a little grumpy (which means she's starving too).

This is where the last-minute recipe comes in. The next few pages give you options for when you're starving, can't be bothered and have to make something quick with whatever is in your pantry.

(Chana Tarkari) Chickpea Curry

SERVES 4 × ACTIVE/TOTAL TIME 25 MINUTES

People are coming over in 30 minutes. I'm thinking, crap what do I make? This is it. I always have rice. I always have spices. And I almost always have these fresh ingredients: onion, garlic and tomato. It's really tasty too. The chickpeas are soft and creamy; you have this spicy, sweet, slightly acidic tomato sauce; it's high in protein and nutrition; and it's very comforting.

2 tablespoons light olive oil
1 brown or red onion,
    thinly sliced
8 garlic cloves, crushed, or
    2 tablespoons garlic
    paste (page 59)
1 teaspoon ground turmeric
1 teaspoon ground coriander
1 teaspoon ground cumin
½ teaspoon smoked paprika
½ teaspoon chilli powder
400 g (14 oz) can diced
    tomatoes
400 g (14 oz) can chickpeas,
    rinsed and drained (see tip)

TO SERVE
1 small bunch of fresh
    coriander (cilantro), leaves
    and stems roughly chopped
Roti (page 57) and Rice
    (page 28)

Heat the oil in a frying pan over medium heat, then add the onion and cook until translucent and slightly golden brown. Add the garlic and the spices and cook until fragrant and the garlic has lost its raw edge, 2–3 minutes. Add the tomatoes and one-quarter can full of water (put some water in the tomato can, swirl it around and use that to get extra tomato juices). Bring to a simmer and, while stirring constantly, cook for 5 minutes (it should slightly thicken).

Add the chickpeas and season with salt to taste. Cook for another 5–10 minutes until the chickpeas have slightly softened (you want some chew, not complete mush) and they've had a chance to absorb all that flavour.

Take off the heat, sprinkle with fresh coriander and serve with roti and rice.

TIP Dried or canned chickpeas? I've tried both and they're very similar. Dried are cheaper and slightly better, but you just save so much time with canned chickpeas. For the amount of time you save, it's worth the extra cost, which is a negligible difference anyway.

10-Minute Chilli Peanut/Sesame Noodles

SERVES 2 × ACTIVE/TOTAL TIME 10 MINUTES

This is super easy to make. I've made it a game to see how quickly I can do it. My record is 7 minutes.

1 teaspoon grapeseed oil
250 g (9 oz) minced
    (ground) pork (see tip)
1 teaspoon soy sauce
Pinch of ground white pepper
400 g (14 oz) whatever
    fresh noodles you like
    (I go for udon)

SAUCE

2 tablespoons smooth peanut
    butter or tahini
1 tablespoon chilli oil
1 tablespoon light soy sauce
2 teaspoons black vinegar (rice
    wine vinegar can work too)
3 garlic cloves, crushed, or
    1½ teaspoons garlic
    paste (page 59)
¼ teaspoon caster (superfine)
    sugar
¼ teaspoon MSG or chicken
    stock (bouillon) powder
    (see tip)
¼ teaspoon ground
    white pepper

TO SERVE

2 spring onions (scallions),
    thinly sliced (optional)
Chilli oil or sliced fresh
    red chilli

Get a saucepan of water boiling. Heat the grapeseed oil in a frying pan over high heat, then spread the pork over the base of the pan as evenly as you can. Let that one side cook until browned and crispy, about 3–5 minutes. Add the soy sauce and white pepper and give it a stir. Cook for another 3–5 minutes. You want to cook it further than you might think. (You're not going for a juicy or tender pork, you want a dry, crispy texture.)

If you're confident, while the pork is cooking, mix all the sauce ingredients in a bowl, then place the noodles in the saucepan of boiling water. Cook according to packet instructions. When they're done, reserve ¼ cup (60 ml) of the noodle water, then drain the noodles and add them to the sauce bowl. Add 2–3 tablespoons of reserved noodle water to the bowl and mix, adding more noodle water if necessary.

Plate up by dividing the noodles between serving bowls and topping each with the pork, spring onion, if using, and chilli oil or fresh chilli.

TIPS You can use frozen pork mince for this. I get mince, put it in a ziplock bag, then flatten it out. If you get it really thin, you don't need to thaw it. Just whack it straight in the pan.

To go meat free, sub out the pork for sliced mushrooms, cabbage, broccoli or firm tofu.

If you're using LaoGanma Hot Chilli Oil or another chilli oil with MSG in it, you don't need to add much (if any) MSG to the sauce.

Spicy Prawn Pasta

SERVES 2 × ACTIVE/TOTAL TIME 10 MINUTES

This is a quick weeknight dinner. By the time the pasta boils, the sauce is done. Make it with whatever you have in your pantry — if you don't have miso, use MSG or chicken stock (bouillon) powder. If you don't have white wine vinegar, use another vinegar or fresh lemon.

200 g (7 oz) dried pasta
1 tablespoon light olive oil
3 large garlic cloves,
   thinly sliced
1 bird's eye chilli, thinly sliced
½ teaspoon chilli flakes
2 teaspoons white wine vinegar
½ × 400 g (14 oz) can whole
   peeled tomatoes
1 teaspoon miso paste
200 g (7 oz) peeled raw prawns
   (see tip)
15 g (½ oz) unsalted butter
20 g (¾ oz) parmesan
1 small bunch of fresh flat-leaf
   parsley, leaves finely
   chopped

Bring a saucepan of salted water to the boil, then add the pasta and cook for about 2 minutes less than the packet instructions specify.

Meanwhile, heat the oil in a frying a pan over high heat, then add the garlic, fresh chilli, chilli flakes and a few cracks of black pepper. Once the edges of the garlic just start to go golden brown, about 1–2 minutes, add the vinegar, tomatoes, miso and 2 tablespoons water.

While the sauce comes to a simmer, roughly chop the prawns into 1–2 cm (½–¾ inch) chunks.

Add the prawn to the frying pan and cook for 1–2 minutes. At this point the pasta should be just about done. Reserve ¼ cup (60 ml) of the pasta water, then drain the pasta and transfer it to the frying pan along with the reserved pasta water. Add the butter and grate the parmesan into the sauce, then mix until the sauce thickens slightly. Taste for salt and adjust if need be. Mix in the parsley and serve.

TIP You can use frozen prawns. If you dice them while frozen, they will thaw and cook at the same time. It's no different to using fresh prawn in this recipe.

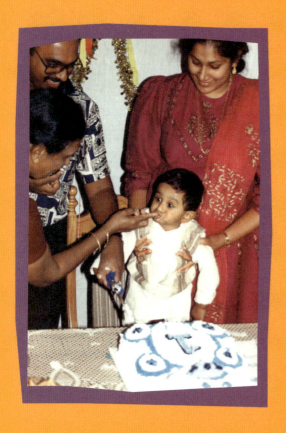

The woman in this photo above is my mum and to the left is my parti (Grandma) feeding me cake at my first birthday — both two of my biggest food influences.

Dessert:
Don't Over-Complicate Things

I think desserts are often over-complicated. I grew up watching Adriano Zumbo and the contestants on *MasterChef* make all these crazy, elaborate desserts. I think restaurants use this course to really push the envelope; they want to give people something to talk about and it's the diner's last impression of the meal. All this can put pressure on the home cook to create these incredibly complicated and aesthetic desserts. But there's a certain science and skill required to make dishes like that. Everything has to be so precise and sometimes you need a bunch of very expensive specialty equipment to make it happen.

I love all that stuff, but when I have people over and it's time for sweets, I don't want to take two days to make it. I don't even want to spend 30 minutes. The max I want to spend is 5 minutes plating something up — what's important is that I get back to hanging out with my guests. The desserts in this chapter are designed for that. You can prep them beforehand, make them in bulk and just take them out of the fridge and plate up when you're ready to roll.

Like all cooking, just try to make it simple and apply the same rules as for savoury food: think about flavour first, then texture, and only after those things think about looks. One of my favourite desserts is a simple fruit platter. Growing up, Mum would always cut up some fruit after dinner — mango and watermelon were the go-tos, but we'd also have tinned fruit with evaporated milk. If guests were coming over, Mum would make payasam too, which is like a milky sago pudding flavoured with cardamom (page 49). But guests or not, there was always a fruit platter. I would argue that there is still skill in making a good one — it's all about sourcing the best fruit, knowing what is seasonal and at its best, and choosing fruit that will perfectly ripen in time for when your guests are coming over. My personal faves are mango and custard apple.

But honestly, my favourite is just a really good quality vanilla bean ice-cream. If I want to be fancy, I'll add lemon curd and crushed-up biscuits for texture, but just plain vanilla bean ice-cream does the job. I serve up a scoop at the end of a meal all the time. It's perfect.

Lychee and Mango Trifles

MAKES 4 MINI TRIFLES × ACTIVE/TOTAL TIME 30 MINUTES + 2 HOURS CHILLING

I love trifles. When I was in primary school, we had show and tell. The assignment was to show a procedure. Everyone did LEGO or some kind of toy assembling. I did trifle. I brought everything in — the sponge, the jelly, the custard — and in front of the whole class, I showed everyone how to assemble a trifle. I felt like I was doing a mini cooking show in primary school, living out my childhood dream as a child.

Years later, I made this recipe. When I started cooking, I was always following recipes or trying to recreate things I'd seen on TV, but this was the first recipe I made up, totally conceived in my mind. It may not be the coolest dish, but it was a pretty significant one in my development.

1 Classic Sponge Cake
   (see tip on page 127 or
   store-bought, if you're
   running short on time),
   at room temperature

LYCHEE CREAM
560 g (1 lb 4 oz) can pitted
   lychees in syrup
300 ml (10½ fl oz) thickened
   (whipping) cream
1 heaped tablespoon (15 g)
   icing (confectioners') sugar
1 teaspoon vanilla bean paste
   or vanilla essence

MANGO FILLING
1 mango (see tip)
2 teaspoons lime juice
   (from about ½ lime),
   plus extra to taste
Icing (confectioners') sugar,
   to taste

To make the lychee cream, drain the lychees into a sieve set over a bowl, reserving the syrup. Press down on the lychees in the sieve to get as much of the syrup out as you can. Blend the lychees in a blender until smooth. In another bowl, using electric beaters or a hand whisk, whip the cream, sugar and vanilla until stiff peaks form. Add the lychee puree and fold through. (The cream should still hold, but give it a little extra whip if it's too loose.)

To make the mango filling, peel the mango and cut the flesh from the seed. Dice the flesh, reserving any juice that comes out. Place the diced mango and reserved juice in a bowl with the lime juice and a pinch of salt. Mix and adjust with extra lime juice and more salt, if you need. (It should be sour at first, then you should have a little bit of saltiness in the background, then a burst of refreshing, sweet mango flavour.) If it needs more sweetness, add a bit of icing sugar.

Cut the sponge cake in half horizontally. (You want it nice and thin.) Pick out four serving glasses (any nice glass or jar you want to serve in) and use the rim of a glass to cut the cake into perfect circles. (You want to end up with eight circle pieces in total. You'll need to cut and combine a few semi-circles.)

Place a layer of sponge at the bottom of each glass. Top each with a generous tablespoon of the reserved lychee syrup, then a generous tablespoon of the mango filling, then about 2 tablespoons of the lychee cream. Repeat layering for a second time, finishing with a little mango filling on top. Place the trifles in the fridge for 2 hours (overnight is fine too). Remove from the fridge 20 minutes before serving.

TIPS Kensington Pride is the best Australian mango, not just for this, but generally. Make these trifles when mangoes are in season and at their best.

You can make a fresh lychee filling instead of mango, but it will take a while to peel and deseed ten of them and be a bit more expensive too. Drizzle some of the reserved lychee syrup over the sponge pieces to soak in before assembling.

Chai Crème Brûlée

SERVES 4 × ACTIVE TIME 15 MINUTES × TOTAL TIME 40 MINUTES
+ 1 HOUR INFUSING AND 5 HOURS SETTING

I friggin' love custard. Growing up we used to get the store-bought stuff or instant powder and I would eat a bowl of it, sometimes as an entire meal. When I first had crème brûlée at a restaurant, I realised it was just a fancy, more acceptable adult version. Also, blowtorching stuff is just cool. When you do it, you'll feel like a chef.

6 g (⅛ oz) fresh ginger, roughly chopped
1 cinnamon stick
7 cardamom pods
3 cloves
1 star anise
1 teaspoon fennel seeds
2 cups (500 ml) thickened (whipping) cream
100 ml (3½ fl oz) milk
10 g (¼ oz) loose Ceylon tea leaves (or from 3–4 teabags)
½ teaspoon vanilla bean paste or vanilla essence
100 g (3½ oz) egg yolks (from about 5 eggs)
50 g (1¾ oz) caster (superfine) sugar
Demerara sugar (or more caster/superfine sugar), for the top (demerara is better if using the oven grill method, see tip)

Use a mortar and pestle to give the ginger and all the spices a rough smash – two to three hits will do the job. (If you don't have a mortar and pestle, smash them with a rolling pin or the back of a big knife.)

Pour the cream and milk into a small saucepan over medium heat, then add the ginger mixture and tea leaves. Stir constantly until you see steam. As soon as you do, take off the heat. (If you have a temperature probe, you want to bring the mixture to 97°C/205°F.) Add the vanilla, mix and allow it to rest and the flavours to infuse for 30 minutes–1 hour.

Preheat the oven to 150°C (300°F). Line a deep baking tray with paper towel (to prevent the ramekins sliding).

Heat the cream mixture back up to 97°C (205°F) or just before it comes to a simmer and keep it at that temperature until you need it in just a minute.

Boil some water in a saucepan. While the water comes to the boil, whisk the egg yolks and caster sugar in a bowl until combined. While whisking constantly, slowly pour the cream mixture over the egg yolk mixture (do a little at a time to ensure the egg yolk doesn't scramble). When combined, pour it through a strainer and into a jug (or any vessel you can pour from easily). Pour the custard mixture into four round ramekins (about 6 cm/2½ inches high, 9 cm/3½ inches deep). Place the custard-filled ramekins in the prepared tray, then pour the boiling water into the tray until it comes about halfway up the side of the ramekins. Carefully place the tray in the oven and bake until the edges of the custard are set and the centre has a slight jiggle, about 35–40 minutes. Allow to cool to room temperature, then place in the fridge for 4–5 hours or overnight to set.

When ready to serve, sprinkle about 1 teaspoon demerara sugar (or caster sugar, see tip) evenly over the top of each custard, then melt using one of the following methods.

OPTION 1: BLOWTORCH
Use a kitchen blowtorch to dissolve the sugar until amber and evenly melted.

OPTION 2: OVEN GRILL
Preheat the oven grill (fan off) to the highest temperature for 5–10 minutes with a rack as high to the grill as you can get. Place the ramekins on a baking tray and under the hot grill, keeping the oven door open. Watch them like a hawk and pull them out as soon as the sugar is melted and bubbly – shouldn't be any longer than 1–2 minutes.

TIPS You can get the caramelised top by using the oven grill instead of a blowtorch, but use demerara sugar. It melts faster, which you need because you don't want the custard in the oven long.

If you want to go classic crème brûlée instead of this chai version, just add 1 teaspoon vanilla bean paste or a freshly scraped vanilla pod instead of the tea and spices.

Dessert Tacos

MAKES 10 × ACTIVE/TOTAL TIME 20 MINUTES + 4–8 HOURS FREEZING

You eat it like a taco, it's a semi-circle like a taco, it kinda looks like a taco, but it isn't a taco. It's an ice-cream sandwich. I got the idea from a taco, so that's why I called it a dessert taco.

It all started when Choco Taco (an American ice-cream in a chocolate-dipped waffle cone shaped like a taco) was discontinued in 2020. Everyone on the internet was talking about it. I'd never had one, but I wanted to make it. First, I tried making the taco shape out of tuile, but it was too fragile. Then, I tried to make a taco out of cookie dough and put ice-cream in it, but it was too hard. The dough kept breaking when I curled it. I made so many cookies that I was sick of it, but the idea was okay. So, I went to the greatest cookie store of all time, Subway, and got two cookies. I used them to sandwich Connoisseur Cookies & Cream ice-cream (the best flavour there is) and dipped it in chocolate, then a peanut chilli crumb. The cookie isn't too hard or too soft, you get the perfect bite, and it holds the ice-cream. The peanut chilli crumb gives it a little something, something.

Do I feel bad when I tell people I made this dessert (because technically I didn't make anything)? Yeah, I kinda do. Do I regret it? Never. I guarantee if you have friends over and you serve them this, one of them will say, 'This is the best thing I've ever had. How did you make this?' Just say it's a secret.

1 litre (640 g) tub cookies and cream or vanilla ice-cream (get the best quality you can)
10 Subway Cookies (any flavour, but I go classic Chocolate Chip)
250 g (9 oz) dark chocolate
15 g (½ oz) coconut oil
200 g (7 oz) roasted peanuts
½ teaspoon chilli powder
½ teaspoon salt

Line a freezerproof tray with baking paper.

Sandwich a scoop of ice-cream between two cookies. Repeat with the remaining cookies and ice-cream. Place on the prepared tray and in the freezer and let them set for 4 hours—overnight (you could honestly stop here and have this as dessert, your mates will love it).

Once they're solid enough to cut in half, cut the ice-cream sandwiches in half, then place them back in the freezer.

Melt the chocolate and coconut oil in a heatproof bowl in the microwave, then allow it to come down to room temperature (should still be melted, just no longer hot).

Meanwhile, blitz the peanuts, chilli and salt in a food processor until you have a rough crumb. Transfer the mixture to a bowl.

Take the ice-cream sandwiches out of the freezer and dip the curved side in the melted chocolate, then in the peanut chilli crumb. Place them on a tray, flat side down, and back in the freezer until you're ready to serve. Remove from the freezer about 2–5 minutes before you're ready to eat, then serve.

Tres Leches Two Ways:
The OG and its Indian Cousin

**SERVES 8–10 × ACTIVE TIME 20 MINUTES × TOTAL TIME 30 MINUTES
+ 1 HOUR STEEPING (FOR RASMALAI) AND OVERNIGHT SOAKING**

The first time I had tres leches was at a Mexican restaurant. It was instantly familiar: the creamy texture, the completely saturated cake, the milkiness. It reminded me of rasmalai, an epic Indian dessert we used to get from the fridges of Indian shops. It's like a little cake dumpling soaked in a saffron and cardamom cream. I don't know how to make rasmalai, I just thought I'd make this — one of the greatest cakes ever — with the flavour of saffron and cardamom that you get in a rasmalai. I've included both the OG and my rasmalai-ish Indian take. Just pick which soak you want, then change the garnish for the soak you've chosen.

1 Classic Sponge Cake (see tip on page 127), still in the cake tin, at room temperature
300 ml (10½ fl oz) thickened (whipping) cream
1 tablespoon icing (confectioners') sugar
1 teaspoon vanilla essence

OG SOAK
395 g (13¾ oz) can sweetened condensed milk
340 ml (11½ fl oz) can evaporated milk
150 ml (5 fl oz) milk
½ teaspoon vanilla bean paste or vanilla essence

RASMALAI SOAK
340 ml (11½ fl oz) can evaporated milk
150 ml (5 fl oz) milk
7–8 green cardamom pods (smashed with a pestle, rolling pin or the side of a knife)
¼ teaspoon saffron threads (10–15 threads)
395 g (13¾ oz) can sweetened condensed milk

TO SERVE
1 tablespoon ground cinnamon (for OG)
OR
1 teaspoon ground cardamom and a few pistachio kernels, roughly chopped (for rasmalai)

OPTION 1: OG
To make the OG tres leches soak, place all the OG soak ingredients in a bowl and whisk until smooth, then you're good to go.

OPTION 2: RASMALAI
To make the rasmalai soak, heat all the soak ingredients, except the condensed milk, in a small saucepan until 90°C (195°F) or until just before it comes to the boil. Take off the heat and allow it to steep for 1 hour. Strain into a bowl, add the condensed milk and whisk to combine.

Use a fork or skewer to poke as many holes as you can over the entire sponge cake. Give the soak mixture a gentle whisk, then pour half of it over the cake and allow it to soak for 10 minutes. Pour the remaining soak mixture over the cake, cover and place it in the fridge overnight (or 4 hours works if you're short on time, see tip).

Using electric beaters or a hand whisk, whisk the cream, icing sugar and vanilla in a bowl until you have soft peaks. Spread the cream topping over the cake, then top with a dusting of either cinnamon (for OG) or cardamom and pistachio (for rasmalai). Serve the cake at room temperature or cold.

TIP You can get away with a 4-hour soak instead of overnight, but you will have some dry bits. Overnight will give you complete saturation, which is what you want.

Orange and Cardamom Ricotta Cake

SERVES 8 × ACTIVE TIME 20 MINUTES × TOTAL TIME 1 HOUR 20 MINUTES

There is only one word to describe this: moist. When people are coming over and I need a bulk dessert, I often make this. It's inspired by the Italian cake; my twist is adding orange and cardamom. Cardamom is nostalgic for me as it's in a lot of Indian desserts.

160 g (5½ oz) unsalted butter, softened
250 g (9 oz) raw caster (superfine) sugar
400 g (14 oz) ricotta
1 teaspoon vanilla bean paste or vanilla essence
3 eggs, at room temperature
1 orange, zested and juiced
200 g (7 oz) plain (all-purpose) flour
2 teaspoons ground cardamom
1 teaspoon baking powder

TO SERVE
1 tablespoon icing (confectioners') sugar
Vanilla ice-cream

Preheat the oven to 180°C (360°F). Line the base and side of a 22 cm (8½ inch) springform cake tin with baking paper. (You can use a regular cake tin, the springform just makes it easier to get out.)

Place the butter and caster sugar in a stand mixer fitted with a paddle attachment. Beat until light and fluffy (you should see and feel minimal grains of sugar). If you don't have a stand mixer or electric beaters, you can do this with a firm spatula and some determination. Add the ricotta and mix. With the mixer running, pour in the vanilla, then the eggs, one at a time and only adding the next one once the egg is completely incorporated. Add the orange zest and juice. With the mixer still running, sift in the flour, cardamom and baking powder. Once combined, pour the cake batter into the prepared tin and bake until a skewer comes out clean, about 45–50 minutes. Allow the cake to cool (not completely, it's nice to have it a little warm, see tip).

Garnish the cake by sprinkling or sifting over the icing sugar, slice and serve with ice-cream.

TIP If you've made this ahead of time, microwave slices before serving to get it nice and warm. It's a nice contrast with the ice-cream.

Buttermilk Panna Cotta

SERVES 4 × ACTIVE TIME 15 MINUTES × TOTAL TIME 15 MINUTES + 4 HOURS SETTING

I always remember my tata (grandpa) drinking buttermilk. On a hot summer's day or after dinner, he'd just sip away at a whole glass. As a kid I thought it was disgusting. What the hell is this thick milk-yoghurt thing? I thought other Indians must be drinking it too, but it was just Tata.

I've grown to really love the taste and texture of it, and I've tried to incorporate it in a few desserts as a nod to my grandpa. This is a classic panna cotta, with the buttermilk giving a silky texture and cheesecake-like flavour. It also makes the whole process quicker as it cools down faster — just four or five hours to set. I also really love desserts that aren't too sweet, so this is right on the money for me. Fresh fruit is my favourite topping. When mangoes are in season, they're a killer topping. Figs too.

2 teaspoons powdered gelatine
1 cup (250 ml) thickened (whipping) cream
120 g (4¼ oz) raw caster (superfine) sugar
2 cups (500 ml) buttermilk
1 teaspoon vanilla bean paste or vanilla essence
Your favourite fruit, sliced

Place the gelatine in a small bowl with 2 teaspoons water and set aside for 5 minutes to bloom (a fancy way of saying, make sure the gelatine is fully hydrated).

Place the cream and sugar in a saucepan over medium heat, stirring constantly, until it gets to the point just before boiling (you'll start to see steam rising from the pan). Mix in the bloomed gelatine mixture, stirring, until the sugar and gelatine have dissolved. Take the pan off the heat, transfer the mixture to a bowl and allow it to cool slightly.

Add the buttermilk and vanilla to the bowl. Stir well, then pour the liquid into your desired serving vessel. Place in the fridge for a minimum of 4 hours to set (overnight is fine if you want to make it the day before).

Serve topped with your favourite fruit.

Margarita Three Ways

Margarita is my favourite cocktail. It always feels like a party or a celebration. Surprisingly, they're sick with Indian food.

Passionfruit Margarita

SERVES 1 × ACTIVE/TOTAL TIME 5 MINUTES

2 passionfruit
45 ml (1½ fl oz) tequila
20 ml (½ fl oz) triple sec
20 ml (½ fl oz) orange juice (from about ½ orange)
15 ml (½ fl oz) agave nectar or simple sugar
    syrup (page 212)
1 teaspoon salt

SALT RIM
1 lime wedge
Flaky sea salt

Salt the rim of a cocktail glass using the lime wedge and flaky sea salt (see tip).

Scoop out the pulp from 1 passionfruit and add it to a cocktail shaker with ice cubes (see tip). Add the remaining ingredients and shake for 30 seconds. Fill the prepared glass with plenty of ice cubes, then strain the margarita into the glass. Garnish with the scooped-out pulp from the remaining passionfruit.

Jalapeño Margarita

SERVES 1 × ACTIVE/TOTAL TIME 5 MINUTES

60 ml (2 fl oz) tequila
30 ml lime juice (from about 2 limes)
20 ml (½ fl oz) orange juice (from about ½ orange)
15 ml (½ fl oz) agave nectar or simple sugar
    syrup (page 212)
¼ jalapeño chilli, cut into 5–6 thin slices,
    plus 3–4 slices extra

CHILLI SALT RIM
1 teaspoon chilli flakes
1 teaspoon flaky sea salt
1 lime wedge

To make the chilli salt rim, mix the chilli flakes and flaky sea salt on a plate, then salt the rim of a cocktail glass using the lime wedge and chilli salt mixture (see tip).

Place the tequila, lime and orange juice, agave or sugar syrup and jalapeño in a cocktail shaker with ice cubes (see tip) and shake for 30 seconds. Fill the prepared glass with plenty of ice cubes, then strain the margarita into the glass and garnish with extra jalapeño.

Tamarind Margarita

SERVES 1 × ACTIVE/TOTAL TIME 5 MINUTES

60 ml (2 fl oz) tequila
20 ml (½ fl oz) lime juice (from about 1 lime)
20 ml (½ fl oz) orange juice (from about ½ orange)
15 ml (½ fl oz) agave nectar or simple sugar
    syrup (page 212)
2 teaspoons tamarind paste
1 teaspoon chilli flakes
1 teaspoon salt

CHILLI SALT RIM
1 teaspoon chilli flakes
1 teaspoon flaky sea salt
1 lime wedge

To make the chilli salt rim, mix the chilli and flaky
sea salt on a plate, then salt the rim of a cocktail
glass using the lime wedge and chilli salt mixture
(see tip).

Place the tequila, lime and orange juice, agave or
sugar syrup, tamarind, chilli and salt in a cocktail
shaker with ice cubes (see tip) and shake for
30 seconds. Fill the prepared glass with plenty
of ice cubes, then strain the margarita into
the glass.

TIPS To salt the rim, rub a
wedge of lime around the edge
of the cocktail glass, then dip the
glass in a shallow bowl of salt.
Use a nice flaky sea salt.

If you don't have a shaker, use a
jug and vigorously stir. Same as
the shaker, your goal is not just
to mix, but to cool the drink and
melt a bit of the ice to dilute
the cocktail.

Tamarind
Margarita
(page 209)

Jalapeño
Margarita
(page 208)

Passionfruit
Margarita
(page 208)

Passionfruit
Lemonade
(page 212)

Horchata
(page 213)

Passionfruit Lemonade

Like in those weird, corny family movies, during summer we always had a jug of fresh lemonade in the fridge. It's like the childhood equivalent of a cold beer. When passionfruit were in season (we had a vine in the backyard), Mum and Parti (Grandma) would put passionfruit pulp in the lemonade. If it wasn't passionfruit season it was straight lemonade.

1 cup (220 g) caster
   (superfine) sugar
120 ml (3¾ fl oz) passionfruit
   pulp (from about
   10 passionfruit)
600 ml (21 fl oz) sparkling
   water if you're fancy
   (or just use still)
120 ml (3¾ fl oz) lemon juice
   (from about 3 lemons)

To make a simple sugar syrup, cook the sugar and 1 cup (250 ml) water in a saucepan over high heat until the sugar is dissolved. Take off the heat and wait for it to cool.

Meanwhile, mix the passionfruit pulp, sparkling water and most of the lemon juice in a jug.

To the jug add about 120 ml (3¾ fl oz) sugar syrup to taste. If you need more sourness, add some of the remaining lemon juice. Serve with plenty of ice cubes.

TIP You can skip the passionfruit to make a classic lemonade.

As pictured on page 211

Horchata: The OG and Cardamom Spiced

SERVES 4 (MAKES 1.2 LITRES/42 FL OZ) × **ACTIVE/TOTAL TIME 10 MINUTES + OVERNIGHT SOAKING**

I can't remember the restaurant for the life of me, but I remember their horchata. It was this creamy, sweet and slightly savoury milk drink. It was the first time I'd tried it, but it was so familiar — cinnamon spiced and sweet, milky flavours. It's like the Indian drinks and desserts I grew up with.

There are instant horchatas, but I find the powders and syrups don't always mix well and, while good, they don't have the texture of a homemade version. This recipe is so easy and cheap to make, it's worth the extra effort, which is really just putting stuff in a blender. For even deeper pleasure, give it an Indian twist with the cardamom-spiced option.

1 cup (200 g) white long-grain rice
½ cup (80 g) whole almonds
340 ml (11½ fl oz) can evaporated milk
½ × 395 g (13¾ oz) can condensed milk
200 ml (7 fl oz) extra creamy milk (Jersey is best)

FOR THE OG, ADD:
2 cinnamon sticks
Ground cinnamon, to serve

FOR CARDAMOM SPICED, ADD:
1 cinnamon stick
12 cardamom pods
Ground cardamom, to serve

OPTION 1: THE OG
Place the rice, almonds, cinnamon sticks and 3 cups (750 ml) water in a bowl or container, cover and set aside at room temperature to soak overnight.

OPTION 2: CARDAMOM SPICED
Place the rice, almonds, cinnamon stick, cardamom and 3 cups (750 ml) water in a bowl or container, cover and set aside at room temperature to soak overnight.

The next morning, strain the rice mixture and transfer to a blender with the evaporated milk, condensed milk, regular milk and 2 cups (500 ml) water. Blend until super smooth, about 5 minutes.

To serve, generously fill glasses with ice, pour in the horchata, then sprinkle with ground cinnamon or cardamom (see tip).

TIP If you're feeling it, add a shot of vodka per serve.

As pictured on page 211 **EVERYTHING IS INDIAN**

CONDIMENTS

Condiments are a crazy good flavour and time hack. If you're ever short on time, you can just grab a condiment and build a dish around it. A good condiment is a flavour bomb that can also transform any dish you've made. In Indian food, condiments are really important, but we don't call them condiments or think about them like that; they're just part of the cuisine. My grandma and my mum would always have a cupboard full of them, an arsenal of flavours they could use at any time. Every meal they'd get out the rosella leaf chutney, pickled chillies, pickled cumquats or whatever they'd recently made. They'd put them out on the table or kitchen bench, and you'd add one or two of them to your rice and curry, and they'd completely change the meal.

The most nostalgic one for me is pickled chilli. When I was a kid, we had a chilli bush out the front of the house. My grandpa, who would have been about 70 at the time, would pick a chilli off the bush and eat it. I was six and, wanting to copy him, would always grab one and eat it too. My grandma would pickle those chillies in vinegar and a little bit of salt, and he'd eat that with almost every meal. It's the first condiment I remember transforming a meal. Imagine having a rich curry, full of spices, then you have a bite of this sharp, acidic, spicy pickle. It transforms your palate for two or three bites, then mellows out again. I'm describing it in a very cheffy way, but when I was a kid, I just ate it and loved it.

My gateway into making condiments was mayo. When I was a teen, it was hard to find whole egg mayo, so I tried making it myself. It was fascinating. You have these two raw ingredients (egg and oil), which are disgusting to eat on their own, but blend them together and they emulsify and transform. I remember thinking, how does this work? It's incredible. And it only takes 30 seconds. It made me think about food and ingredients in a totally different way.

I started thinking about hot sauces and condiments I'd seen on TV. I experimented with things like salsa macha and suddenly I was enjoying condiments you can't even get in Australia. Then I was adding the hot sauce I made to mayo, and I was eating this super unique sauce, and my friends would be asking me, 'What is this? Why does this taste so good?' It may have blown their minds but it only took me mere seconds to put together and serve with chips. That's the main feature of a condiment for me: the working time is very little, but the flavour is massive.

My tip is don't force a condiment. Make mango pickles when mangoes are in season and cheap, and make lemon curd when there are a lot of lemons. Just like Italians making passata, they do it when the tomatoes are at their peak. You get the best quality, and you save your money.

Chilli Chutney (Mircha Chutney)

MAKES ABOUT 350 G (12 OZ) × ACTIVE/TOTAL TIME 40 MINUTES

This is the recipe that means the most to me. It is the most important condiment I have in my house. It was part of the dish that got me into *MasterChef* and it was my favourite thing Parti (Grandma) made for my family.

Before I went on *MasterChef*, I called her and asked her how she made it. This is how it started:

Me: Grandma, how do you make chilli chutney?

Parti: You put chilli and garlic in.

Then I'd taste a bit from the jar I have.

Me: Okay, but did you put ginger in it too?

Parti: Oh yeah, put ginger in.

Then I look at it.

Me: It's got cumin seeds.

Parti: Oh yeah, it's got cumin seeds. Put that in.

Me: Alright, what about the sourness at the end? What do you put in for that? Lemon or vinegar?

Parti: Lemon.

Me: Okay, coo—

Parti: And sometimes vinegar.

I was thinking, what the heck is this recipe?

Me: Alright, next time you cook it, tell me and I'll come over and I'll watch you do it.

So, I went over with a notepad and watched her do it. I didn't weigh it or anything, I was just watching the technique. I came over a second time to get the right amounts of each ingredient. It was difficult because she had no measurements, she would just do it by taste — she would even know how to season it just by the smell. Then I made a third batch with her just to make sure I'd nailed the recipe. It's the closest I've ever got to making a chutney as good as hers. I gave her a jar and kept one myself.

Little did I know that was the last batch I'd ever make with her. A year later she passed away.

If I ever have a restaurant, Parti's chilli chutney will be on the menu always, in some shape or form. It will be a way for her to be part of the restaurant and for the world to remember her.

If you make one recipe, I hope it's this one. Even if you don't like chilli, just make it anyway because Parti would have loved that.

My family would use it in the traditional way: to just add a bit of chilli to some rice and curry, or by putting a little bit in some roti and wrapping something up in it. Parti would bang it into the base of a curry too. I use it in as many things as I can. It's a killer marinade. I blend it with olive oil and toss it over raw fish. Combine it with butter and pour it over razor clams, lobster or roast fish. Little dollops of it go great on a margherita pizza. I've blended it with vinegar and strained it to make a Tabasco-like hot sauce with a curry-ish vibe. I also have it straight with eggs, chips or fried chicken, and I add it to burgers and cheese toasties. There are a million different things you can do with it, and you'll have a new dish every time.

10 bird's eye chillies
5 large red chillies
2 garlic cloves, roughly chopped
10 g (¼ oz) fresh ginger, finely chopped
5 fresh curry leaves
1 teaspoon cumin seeds
¼ cup (60 ml) mustard oil
1 teaspoon salt
¼ cup (60 ml) lemon juice (from about 2–3 lemons)
1 teaspoon ground cumin
2 tablespoons white vinegar

Blitz all the chillies in a food processor, then add the garlic, ginger, curry leaves and cumin seeds. Blitz again until everything is finely chopped but not pureed. Tip the mixture into a small saucepan. Add the oil and salt to the pan and cook, stirring constantly, over low heat until the sauce thickens and emulsifies, around 20–30 minutes.

Add the lemon juice and cook for another 5 minutes. Add the ground cumin and vinegar. Taste and adjust as needed. (It should be spicy and a little bit sour and salty.)

TIP This chutney will keep in the fridge for 4–6 months.

Left to Right
Top row: Fresh Coriander
Chutney, Aioli, Mexican Chilli Oil.
Middle row: Herb Mayo,
Chilli Chutney, Classic Mayo,
Curry Leaf Butter.
Bottom row: Roasted Garlic
Mayo, Hot Sauce Mayo,
Chilli Chutney Butter.

Lemon Curd

MAKES 350 G (12 OZ) × ACTIVE/TOTAL TIME 15 MINUTES + 4 HOURS–OVERNIGHT SETTING

Honestly, I only got the idea to make this because my auntie would bring over huge amounts of lemons. Usually, we'd make pickles, but I wanted to do something different. What the heck is there? Lemon curd.

Treat it like a spread or jam — try it on toast, banana bread and scones. Or, use it to make a quick dessert: lightly whip some cream, fold through lemon curd, then top with whatever fruit is in season, as well as some crushed-up cookies or meringue (store-bought is good). Or you can always just drizzle it over vanilla ice-cream.

2 eggs
100 g (3½ oz) caster
  (superfine) sugar
65 g (2¼ oz) unsalted butter
  (the best quality, it makes
  a difference)
100 ml (3½ fl oz) lemon juice
  (from about 4–5 lemons)

Whisk the eggs and sugar in a bowl until combined. Pour some water into the bottom saucepan of a double boiler and bring to a simmer over low heat. Place the butter and lemon juice in the top saucepan and set over the pan of simmering water. Once the butter has melted, slowly pour the mixture over the egg mixture while whisking, making sure the egg doesn't scramble.

When combined, pour the mixture back into the top of the double boiler. Bring to a simmer over low heat and cook until thickened. (You want the consistency of runny, squeezy bottle honey.) Transfer to a blender and blitz until it becomes slightly paler and creamier. Pour into a clean jar and chill in the fridge for 4 hours or overnight.

TIPS This curd will keep in the fridge for a few weeks.

You can use this as the filling for the Victoria Sponge (page 126) instead of jam.

As pictured on page 225

Peanut Chutney

MAKES 200 G (7 OZ) × **ACTIVE/TOTAL TIME 5 MINUTES**

This is like Indian peanut butter if peanut butter was super spicy, garlicky, a little sour and salty, and you ate it with curry instead of toast and jam. It's really nothing like peanut butter at all, is it? Traditionally in South India (where my family is from), it would be eaten with dosa (crispy fermented rice pancake) and idli (steamed fermented rice cake), but that got lost in migration (and translation). We ended up having it with rice and roti. I also love it on a taco, spread over or added on top. It's great with Chicken Curry Tacos (page 136), Roti (page 57), pita bread, dosa or idli. There's actually a Mexican peanut salsa (salsa de cacahuate), which is very similar.

130 g (4½ oz) unsalted peanuts (see tip)
30 g (1 oz) sesame seeds
½ brown onion, roughly chopped
2 teaspoons tamarind paste (see tip)
1 tablespoon lemon juice (from about ½ lemon)
3 bird's eye chillies, roughly chopped
4 garlic cloves, roughly chopped

Toast the peanuts and sesame seeds until the sesame seeds are golden brown. Transfer to a blender with the remaining ingredients and ½ cup (125 ml) water and blend until you get close to the consistency of smooth peanut butter. Add more water if you need to thin the chutney. Season with salt to taste.

TIPS If you've got peanut butter in the cupboard, you can use that instead of whole peanuts.

If you have lemon but not tamarind, that's another substitution you can make; just add a bit more lemon than you would tamarind.

This chutney will keep in the fridge for 4–5 days.

As pictured on page 225 | **EVERYTHING IS INDIAN**

Coriander Chutneys

ACTIVE/TOTAL TIME 5 MINUTES

We usually make two versions: a creamy yoghurt chutney and a fresh, light and zingy one, which is very similar to a salsa. I like the creamy one with curry, dhokla and samosa. The fresh one is amazing as a side or as a fresh punch of flavour on Cassava Chips (page 33) or a warm roti, again much like a salsa.

(Dhaniya and Pudina Chutney)

CORIANDER, MINT AND YOGHURT CHUTNEY

1 small bunch of fresh coriander (cilantro), leaves and stems roughly chopped
1 small bunch of fresh mint, leaves picked
1 long green chilli
1–2 garlic cloves, crushed, or 1 teaspoon garlic paste (page 59)
5 g (⅛ oz) fresh ginger, finely grated, or ½ teaspoon ginger paste (page 59)
1 tablespoon extra virgin olive oil
300 g (10½ oz) Greek-style yoghurt

MAKES 320 G (11¼ OZ)

Place all the ingredients, except the yoghurt, in a food processor. Add about 2 tablespoons yoghurt and blitz until smooth. Fold in the remaining yoghurt. (This will give you a thicker texture.) Season with salt to taste.

TIP This chutney will keep in the fridge for up to 3 days.

(Fresh Dhaniya Chutney)

FRESH CORIANDER CHUTNEY

1 small bunch of fresh coriander (cilantro)
1 tomato
½ brown onion
2 garlic cloves
2 bird's eye chillies

MAKES 200 G (7 OZ)

Roughly chop all the ingredients, then place in a blender with a generous pinch of salt. Pulse until well combined.

TIP This chutney will keep in the fridge for up to 2 days.

Clockwise from top right:
Lemon Curd, Coriander,
Mint and Yoghurt Chutney,
Peanut Chutney.

Whole Egg Mayo

Back when I was a teen (this was like ten to fifteen years ago), it was hard to find whole egg mayonnaise. The brand of normal mayo we used to get was … I'll be nice and just say it wasn't very good. It always tasted so oily. When I made mayo for the first time, I realised how much better it could be, like mind-blowingly better.

Now, there are some pretty good store-bought mayos, like Hellmann's, S&W and Best Foods, but I still make it at home. It's a better flavour and texture, and you can control how salty and sour you want it to be. It's also quick to make and, if you're making it in bulk, you always have it in your fridge.

Classic Mayo

MAKES 1 CUP (250 ML)
ACTIVE/TOTAL TIME 5 MINUTES

1 egg
1 teaspoon Dijon mustard
1 cup (250 ml) grapeseed oil
1 tablespoon lemon juice (from about ½ lemon)

Place all the ingredients and a generous pinch of salt in the canister for a stick blender, then blend slowly, lifting slowly and pulsing, until everything is thick and creamy. (Alternatively, use a whisk. Place the egg and mustard in a bowl then very slowly drizzle in the oil while whisking constantly until thick and creamy. Whisk in the lemon juice.) Taste and add more salt if it needs it.

Vegan Mayo

MAKES 1 CUP (250 ML)
ACTIVE/TOTAL TIME 5 MINUTES

50 ml (1½ fl oz) aquafaba (the liquid drained from a 400 g/14 oz can chickpeas)
1 teaspoon Dijon mustard
1 tablespoon white vinegar or lemon juice (from about ½ lemon)
1 cup (250 ml) grapeseed oil

Place all the ingredients, except the oil, and a pinch of salt in a blender. While slowly blending, drizzle in the oil until all the oil has been incorporated and you start to see it thicken and become super creamy.

TIPS To adjust the consistency for both the classic and vegan mayos, thin by mixing in a touch of water or thicken by slowly drizzling in a little more oil while blending.

These mayos will keep in the fridge for up to 1 month.

As pictured on pages 220–221

Flavoured Mayos

Whether you use store-bought or homemade mayo, try blending in some flavours. Fat is a good carrier of flavour, and mayo is mainly fat. So, if you add jalapeño and lime juice, it will preserve and carry that flavour really well. You will also have a spicy mayo that's unique to you. Anywhere you would add mayo, use a flavoured mayo instead and it'll be awesome. Add it to a BLT, a taco, a sandwich or as a dressing for a salad. Even if you just drizzle over chips, it'll blow people's minds and it will have taken just four seconds to throw together.

All the below ingredients can be blended with the Classic Mayo ingredients (opposite), with a finished mayo or a store-bought mayo. These are my suggestions, but you can put anything in. Be creative, a unique condiment really can make a dish.

Aioli

Blend 1–2 crushed garlic cloves into the mayo.

Roasted Garlic Mayo

Preheat the oven to 180°C (360°F). Cut off and discard the top of a whole head of garlic. Place the head on a sheet of foil (big enough to wrap up the garlic). Drizzle over light olive oil and add a pinch of salt, then wrap up tightly in the foil. Roast for 35 minutes. Take out of the oven and allow it to cool. Unwrap the foil, then squeeze each garlic clove from its skin into a blender. Add the mayo and blend.

Hot Sauce Mayo

Pick your favourite hot sauce – sriracha is a classic – and stir 50 ml (1½ fl oz) of it through the mayo.

Herb Mayo

You can use any fresh herbs for this. Bring a saucepan of water to the boil over high heat. Meanwhile, prepare a bowl of ice water. When the water is boiling, blanch the herbs (stems and leaves) for about 10–15 seconds (soft herbs like oregano probably only need 5 seconds, you have to feel it), then immediately transfer them to the ice water to stop the cooking. When they're cool, remove from the ice water and dry with paper towel, a tea (dish) towel or a salad spinner. Blend the herbs (stems and leaves) with the mayo.

Jalapeño and Lime Mayo

Blend 2 roughly chopped jalapeño chillies and the juice of 1 lime into the mayo.

How to Pickle Anything

MAKES ENOUGH FOR A 2 CUP (500 ML) MASON JAR × ACTIVE/TOTAL TIME 5 MINUTES + 2 HOURS PICKLING

Indians love pickles. Unsurprisingly, we usually go heavy on the spice and garlic. At home, we would make them from whatever was in season or growing in the garden. If it was summer, we'd be making mango achar. If chillies were abundant, chilli pickle. Sometimes my aunties would come over with a big bag of cumquats, lemons or whatever was growing in their garden. Our first thought was always to make a pickle.

Having pickles in your cupboard is like having acidity and texture you can access at any time. Finely chop some and put them in a salad, add them to a taco, put a heap in a burger, have them with fried chicken or curry, or add pickled fruit to a dessert. It's a killer hack.

The recipe is the same for any fruit or vegetable. My favourite things to pickle are green chilli, red onion, cucumber and baby red radish.

Fruit or vegetables (whatever is fresh, in season and cheap), enough to fit in a mason jar

PICK YOUR FLAVOURINGS
(Honestly, be creative, whatever goes)
Whole black peppercorns
Coriander seeds
Mustard seeds
Fennel seeds
Fresh herbs
Citrus peel

THE BASE
200 ml (7 fl oz) white vinegar
1 tablespoon (20 g) salt
2 teaspoons (10 g) caster (superfine) sugar

Wash and slice the fruit or vegetables as thin or thick as you desire, then pack them into a clean mason jar. If you want to add flavour, my guide is to start with at least ½ teaspoon of each spice. If you're using fresh herbs, a small handful of each. If you're using citrus peel, use 2–3 wide strips.

Place all the base ingredients and 200 ml (7 fl oz) water in a small saucepan and simmer until the sugar and salt is dissolved. Pour the liquid into the jar over the fruit or veg. Ensure all the ingredients are fully submerged in the pickling liquid. If they aren't submerged, fold up a paper towel and soak it in some white vinegar and place it over the fruit or veg so it's covering them. Place the jar in the fridge for about 2 hours and you're good to go.

TIP This pickle will keep in the fridge for up to 6 months.

Chicken Salt

MAKES 100 G (3½ OZ) × ACTIVE/TOTAL TIME 5 MINUTES

In primary school, whenever we had a birthday or something special happened, we'd get some lunch money from Dad. Our school didn't have a canteen, but there was a chip shop next door. The ultimate lunch order was a bag of chips for $3.50, with chicken salt and barbecue sauce, all wrapped up in butcher's paper. You'd get a large and everyone would be there asking for a chip. You'd make friends.

That smell and flavour is something all Australians grow up with and it's about time the world knew. This recipe is the grown-up version of that flavour. The texture is like KFC salt: very powdery, but I really like it because it just melts into a hot chip. Think of it as something that goes on more than just chips. I've used it to season roast vegetables, roast chicken (it gives you that supermarket rotisserie chicken flavour) and steak.

2 tablespoons chicken stock
    (bouillon) powder
¼ teaspoon garlic powder
½ teaspoon onion powder
⅛ teaspoon citric acid
½ teaspoon caster (superfine)
    sugar
Pinch of smoked paprika
Pinch of ground turmeric
2 tablespoons salt

Use a spice grinder, blender or mortar and pestle to blitz all the ingredients until you have a fine powder. (If you really can't be bothered, just mix everything in a bowl.)

TIP This salt will keep in the pantry for 4–6 months.

Curry Leaf and Chilli Chutney Compound Butters

MAKES 130 G (4½ OZ) × ACTIVE/TOTAL TIME 5 MINUTES

Compound butters are just butter with flavours mixed in. They're super easy to make and can transform a piece of seafood, pizza or even just toast. The idea for this came during Christmas a few years ago. My family home always had an abundance of curry leaves on the tree — I'm talking thousands of leaves, but we only use around ten in a recipe. I was thinking, what could we do with them all? I also wanted to make curry leaves the hero flavour, rather than the sidekick, which is how they're usually treated. So, I blended a heap of them with some butter, lathered a fish in it and roasted it, then I did another fish with the same idea but with chilli chutney instead of curry leaves.

CURRY LEAF BUTTER
125 g (4½ oz) unsalted butter,
    softened (see tip)
150–200 fresh curry leaves
    (from about 10 sprigs)
2 garlic cloves, roughly
    chopped
5 g (⅛ oz) fresh ginger
1 green chilli, roughly chopped
½ teaspoon ground cumin
½ teaspoon ground coriander
1 teaspoon lime juice
    (from about ¼ lime)

Blitz all the ingredients and a generous pinch of salt in a food processor until smooth.

CHILLI CHUTNEY BUTTER
125 g (4½ oz) unsalted butter,
    softened (see tip)
1 tablespoon Chilli Chutney
    (page 218)

Blitz the butter and chutney in a food processor until smooth.

TIPS Use the best quality butter you can find. My favourite is Beurre d'Isigny AOP Unsalted Butter, a French butter sold at specialty grocers, like Harris Farm.

Store these compound butters in the fridge, wrapped in baking paper or in an airtight container for 1–2 weeks.

As pictured on pages 220–221

Mexican Chilli Oil (Salsa Macha)

MAKES 2 CUPS (500 ML) × ACTIVE TIME 20 MINUTES × TOTAL TIME 35 MINUTES

Salsa macha is the Mexican cousin of Chinese crispy chilli oil. I discovered it when I was diving into Mexican food and have been making it ever since. The dried chillies, which are always in my pantry, have so much nuance and flavour. It's different to a chilli oil because it's not too spicy; you get texture from all the nuts and seeds, and it's got this slight sweetness as well.

I put it on eggs, in tacos, over grilled chicken or seafood and swirled through pumpkin (squash) soup. Try roast vegetables with it: just a little pinch of salt and a bit of oil, roast until they're a little caramelised, then add a whole heap of salsa macha to dress it. Because it's perfectly seasoned — sweet, sour, salty and spicy — your roast veg will have this complex flavour and it's all from a condiment you can just chuck on.

2 cups (500 ml) light olive oil
4 garlic cloves, thinly sliced
2 dried ancho chillies, seeded and roughly chopped
2 dried guajillo chillies, seeded and roughly chopped
5 dried morita chillies, seeded and roughly chopped
1–2 chile de árbol chillies, seeded and roughly chopped
¼ cup (40 g) roasted almonds
1 teaspoon sesame seeds
1 teaspoon coriander seeds
½ teaspoon cumin seeds
1 teaspoon soft brown sugar, plus extra to taste
1 teaspoon apple cider vinegar, plus extra to taste
½ teaspoon salt, plus extra to taste

Place the oil and garlic in a small saucepan and bring to a simmer over low heat until the garlic just turns golden brown, about 5 minutes. Take off the heat and, while the oil is still hot, mix in the chillies, almonds, sesame, coriander and cumin seeds. Allow it to cool for 10–15 minutes, then mix in the sugar, vinegar and salt.

Pour the mixture into a food processor and pulse until everything is the same-ish size. Taste and season with more salt, sugar and/or vinegar if necessary.

TIP This oil will keep in the pantry for 3–4 months.

ACKNOWLEDGEMENTS

Wow. We wrote a book — I say 'we' because I don't think this would be possible without the incredible people that helped me/us get here.

There are a lot of people I want to acknowledge and express my gratitude to, I feel I could write an entire book just on that.

I wanted to start by firstly thanking my family for putting up with my chaos. Thank you for supporting me in whatever random idea I had, whether it was driving across Australia to move to Perth (thanks Immanuel and Dad), quitting my job to do a TV show, washing dishes after I went on a recipe development rampage (thanks Naomi and Esther), or teaching and encouraging me to cook (thanks Mum, Parti and Tata). Thank you for always supporting me, believing in me and allowing me to chase a dream.

Thank you to my incredible team — special mention to Harrison Little, thank you for your patience.

A huge thank you to Murdoch Books for popping my writer's cherry. Special mentions to Justin Wolfers — great name — thank you for seeing the potential in this and helping to bring it to life. Sarah Odgers — you're a visionary. To Rob Palmer, Lucy Tweed, George Saad, Alex McDivitt, Virginia Birch, Sarah Hatton and the ten other people I forgot to mention (soz), thank you. I am incredibly grateful to you all and thank you for allowing me to bring this to life. It is an honour.

To the one and only Nicholas Jordan. You've got an incredible gift to draw the best out of people and put words, sentences and paragraphs to the random thoughts and conversations we have. I loved every moment.

Lastly, to Mum and Dad, aka Alick and Sunita Narayan. I would not be who I am and do what I do without you. You taught me to dream big, put people first, give them your best and that, with God, nothing is impossible. This book is dedicated to you.

But lastly. . . for real this time, thanks to my stunning, ever-patient and fearless wife. Esther, I will always love you. I love the life we have together, thank you for organising the chaos and bringing the best out of it. What a ride.

Index

Published in 2025 by Murdoch Books, an imprint of Allen & Unwin

Murdoch Books Australia
Cammeraygal Country
83 Alexander Street
Crows Nest NSW 2065
Phone: +61 (0)2 8425 0100
murdochbooks.com.au
info@murdochbooks.com.au

Murdoch Books UK
Ormond House
26–27 Boswell Street
London WC1N 3JZ
Phone: +44 (0) 20 8785 5995
murdochbooks.co.uk
info@murdochbooks.co.uk

For corporate orders and custom publishing, contact our business development team
at salesenquiries@murdochbooks.com.au

Publisher: Justin Wolfers
Editorial Manager: Virginia Birch
Design Manager: Sarah Odgers
Design and illustrations: George Saad Studio
Editor: Alex McDivitt
Photographer: Rob Palmer
Stylist: Lucy Tweed
Writer: Nicholas Jordan
Production Manager: Natalie Crouch

*Murdoch Books acknowledges the Traditional Owners of the Country on which we live and work.
We pay our respects to all Aboriginal and Torres Strait Islander Elders, past and present.*

ISBN 978 1 76150 034 3

 A catalogue record for this
book is available from the
National Library of Australia

A catalogue record for this book is available from the British Library

Colour reproduction by Splitting Image Colour Studio Pty Ltd, Wantirna, Victoria
Printed in China by C&C Offset Printing Co., Ltd.

OVEN GUIDE: You may find cooking times vary depending on the oven you are using.
For fan-forced ovens, as a general rule, set the oven temperature to 20°C (25–50°F)
lower than indicated in the recipe.

TABLESPOON MEASURES: We have used 20 ml (4 teaspoon) tablespoon measures. If you
are using a 15 ml (3 teaspoon) tablespoon add an extra teaspoon of the ingredient for each
tablespoon specified.

10 9 8 7 6 5 4 3 2 1

MIX
Paper | Supporting
responsible forestry
FSC® C008047